A BEGINNER'S GUIDE TO NUMEROLOGY

A BEGINNER'S GUIDE TO
NUMEROLOGY

Decode Relationships, Maximize Opportunities, AND Discover Your Destiny

JOY WOODWARD

CALLISTO PUBLISHING

Copyright © 2019 by Callisto Publishing LLC
Cover and internal design © 2019 by Callisto Publishing LLC
All illustrations used under license from iStock.com.
Author photo courtesy of © Curtis Comeau
Art Director: Antonio Valverde
Art Producer: Sara Feinstein
Editor: Samantha Barbaro
Production Editor: Andrew Yackira

Callisto Publishing and the colophon are registered trademarks of Callisto
Publishing LLC

Published by Callisto Publishing LLC C/O Sourcebooks LLC
P.O. Box 4410, Naperville, Illinois 60567-4410
(630) 961-3900
callistopublishing.com

Printed in the United States of America.
Versa 27

1234567890123456789012345678901234567890123456789012345678901234567890

To my dear husband:

The adventure continues . . .

xox

CONTENTS

4   PERSONAL CYCLES: MAKING THE MOST OUT OF EVERY DAY, MONTH, AND YEAR 69

5   REVEALING CHARTS & ARROWS 93

INTRODUCTION

W hat if I told you there's a tool that can help you understand the motivations of your family, friends, and coworkers and make all your relationships more predictable? This same tool can guide you to harness your intuition and give you more confidence in all of your decisions and life choices. Well, this tool exists. It's called Numerology.

We can choose to go through life either aware or unaware, enlightened or asleep. Numerology can be part of your spiritual awakening, helping you get in touch with your higher self and true purpose.

I discovered the power of Numerology more than a decade ago, when I had my very first reading. It was as if I had been given a decoder ring for my personality and motivations. I finally understood—and had validation for—why I was so sensitive, why I felt responsible for everyone else, and the types of clashes I experienced with teachers and bosses. Immediately after the reading, I purchased my first Numerology book.

Since that day, the system of Numerology has completely changed my life. On a daily basis, it allows me to choose dates, names, projects, and relationships with more confidence. I left behind my longtime corporate career. It was scary, to say the least, but the Universe had other plans.

What started as a cool party trick eventually morphed into a new business. The friends and acquaintances I'd given early unsolicited readings to started insisting on further sessions. They sent their friends and relatives. New clients began to appear. Eventually, I realized what had happened: I had become a Numerologist. Although this was a far cry from the career I had envisioned, I embraced it.

I took certifications and attended workshops and devoured every book I could find on the subject in order to hone my craft. I finally decided it was time to step out of the metaphysical closet. From there, my Numerology business, The Joy of Numerology, was born. I've spent the last decade giving thousands of readings to people from around the world. Every reading reveals more to me and deepens my numerical knowledge. And with this book, I want to share that knowledge with you.

Some people hear "Numerology" and think of complex mathematics. But don't worry! The system requires only simple adding and reducing to a single digit, and I will teach you how to do this.

We'll start with your birth date and the name on your birth certificate. These defining factors hold the secret to decoding your Core Profile, which includes your Soul, Personality, and Destiny Numbers and reveals your karma. During this process, you'll learn all the gifts and meanings behind the day you were born. The influences of your birth date are magical, revelatory, and accurate!

Learning about yourself is the foundation. From there, I'll help you progress to examining your family, friends, partners, and coworkers based on their numbers—and maybe even giving readings to strangers (although no one is really a stranger once you have their numbers!). You'll soon unlock the power of the numbers, which will allow you to improve all your existing relationships—as well as become more discerning about compatibility as you form new relationships. We'll also take a deep dive into the timing and cycles of your Personal Years, Months, and Days, which will guide your decisions and help you plan for the future. Learning Numerology is much like learning a second language. Once you're fluent, your whole perspective will change.

Lastly, without getting too hocus-pocus on you (Numerology is a science, after all), we'll explore other metaphysical arts, such as Tarot, Astrology, Crystals, and Moon Cycles. These all work together, complementing one another and providing deeper insight to the magic of your life.

I've written this book to be accessible to anyone who's interested in exploring and learning about the world of Numerology. If you're a beginner, it has all the information you need to get started. And if you're more experienced (or a professional), I hope you'll find this to be a good refresher that provides some new and intriguing insights.

The book is a thorough guide to this mystical and life-changing tool. You will learn to interpret numbers, create basic charts, and understand the vibrations that make up the energy of your relationships, decisions, and daily life. Are you ready?

Let your numerical adventure begin!

THE STORY BEHIND THE NUMBERS

The first step is understanding what Numerology *is*. Where did this numerical science originate? Let's take a look at a brief history of Numerology, its mystical origins, the tools you'll need to get started, and ways you can use it to examine both yourself and the choices and motivations of others.

What Is Numerology?

Numerology is the study of the mystical relationship between numbers and numerical patterns. It looks at the meaning in the numbers (and letters) in your life. It is an intricate mixture of science, mythology, and philosophy and is a key to decoding the Universe and finding your soul's purpose.

For instance, how often have you, or someone you know, continually seen the same numerical patterns—such as 11:11, 444, or a family member's birthday? These recurring numbers hold messages from the Universe. Numerology will help you tune in to these messages so they can guide your life to its greatest potential.

Similarly, each number on the calendar holds a specific energy. The numbers reveal vibrational themes. Whether it is the 1st, 15th, or 22nd of the month, and depending on where you are in your personal cycle, every date holds a theme and pattern. As you learn about Numerology, you'll begin to see that certain calendar days sync better with your personal energy than others.

Names also hold significance, and you'll learn to interpret the numerical value of letters in your birth name and other names for further discovery.

We'll explore some of the more common numerical patterns throughout this book.

WHAT IS NUMEROLOGY FOR?

Numerology helps you tap into your highest potential. Ultimately, it guides you to better understand yourself and those around you, tap into your intuition, make smarter choices, maximize your potential on certain days and in certain years, understand compatibility with friends and romantic partners, take advantage of auspicious timing, and decide when to act and when to wait. Numerology will lead you to uncover your talents and gifts, understand the cycles of your life, spot Karmic Lessons and Karmic Debt, and embrace change. It reveals the personality traits and potential life obstacles for both you and others and the best actions to take.

Numerology can also help you in looking *back*. When you reflect on the events of your life, the way they unfolded within your numerical cycles will bring clarity to what happened and why.

Knowing what you are meant to be experiencing during a particular year, month, or day makes navigating the cycle of life easier. You'll be able to predict and prepare for upcoming challenges and take advantage of fabulous and rewarding opportunities.

WHAT IS NUMEROLOGY *NOT* FOR?

Numerology is not a crystal ball. Remember that it predicts *potential*. The rest is up to you. Numerology depends on the high and low vibrations of the numbers involved, and its rewards are directly correlated to your efforts. It will not help you win the lottery. (Although many people choose their "lucky numbers" based on birthdays and significant dates.) It will not predict the time or date of your death. (Although it can reveal possible health issues and potential painful cycles in life.)

Numerology provides a framework, but there is always free will and choice involved, as well as environmental factors beyond our control.

Ancient Origins

Although the word *Numerology* did not appear until the early 20th century, evidence of the belief in the metaphysical significance of numbers—generally referred to as "the science of numbers"—can be found throughout history.

Greek philosopher Pythagoras (more on him below) is credited as "the father of numerology." However, numerical significance is noted throughout ancient Egyptian, Babylonian, Asian, and Indian history as well as in many biblical references. Ever since numbers were created, cultures have been applying meaning to them. This continues today.

PYTHAGORAS

Before Socrates, Aristotle, and Plato, there was the Greek philosopher and mystic Pythagoras. His pioneering ideas are the foundation of mathematics, astrology, astronomy, and physics. They include the metaphysics of numbers—the method of viewing numbers not just as amounts and measures but as rates of vibration. His teachings revealed that reality, music, and nature are, in fact, mathematical.

What we know about Pythagoras is part legend and part storytelling. There is no written history of him; firsthand accounts were passed on only through verbal record. He is credited with discovering the science of musical tone, harmony, the musical scale, the Pythagorean theorem, the doctrine of opposites, and, of course, Numerology.

PYTHAGOREAN NUMEROLOGY

Pythagoras developed the concept that every number, no matter how large or small, can always be reduced to a single digit of 1 through 9 and that each reduced digit has a singular cosmic vibration. He applied this to the stages in the human life cycle with eerie accuracy. Pythagorean Numerology is the dominant form of Numerology practiced in the West.

Other forms of Numerology include Chaldean—the most ancient system. It originated in Babylon and is based on the numbers 1 through 8. In this system the number 9 is considered sacred and holy, separate from other vibrations (except when it results as the sum).

The Kabbalah system, which has origins in Hebrew mysticism, focuses only on names and is based on 22 different vibrations of the Hebrew alphabet. A system called New Kabbalah Numerology has been adapted to the Roman alphabet of 26 letters and uses the Pythagorean number chart. This system does not consider the birth date, which is likely why it has never gained popularity among Western Numerologists, as birth date is at the core of Western Numerology.

NUMEROLOGY FOR THE 21ST CENTURY

Mrs. Dow Balliett of Atlantic City is credited with introducing modern Numerology to the Western world. She was part of the New Age Thought Movement of the early 1900s and spread the word of spirituality, enlightenment, and character analysis based on numbers. Her unique teachings were based on the Pythagorean theory of Numerology.

Mrs. Balliett was a significant influence on Dr. Julia Seton, who popularized this system and gave it the modern name of "Numerology." Dr. Seton was an international New Thought lecturer who traveled to many countries and continents teaching the science of names and numbers. Her daughter, Dr. Juno Jordan, continued her legacy.

A dentist by trade, Dr. Jordan had a deep interest in metaphysics and spirituality. She retired her dental tools and founded the California Institute of Numerical Research in the late 1950s. For 25 years she and her colleagues tested numerical theories and patterns. Their conclusion, "NUMBERS DO NOT LIE," is a profound statement that numbers reveal the character and events of the human experience with unfailing accuracy.

These three women had a profound impact on modern Numerology. They defined, shaped, and brought beauty to a science that continues to grow and evolve.

Vibrations in Numbers

Inventor, engineer, and futurist Nikola Tesla said, "If you want to find the secrets of the Universe, think in terms of energy, frequency, and vibration."

Understanding vibration is the foundation for understanding the positive and negative traits of numbers.

Pythagoras's take on vibration was that every object and person contains a spirit force—a primal unseen power from which their momentum and action are born. The higher the spirit force, the more positive the energy or experience; the lower the force, the more negative. You experience these vibrations every day. Having intense chemistry with a person or feeling a strong aversion to a situation— these are vibrations. You've likely heard the expression "your vibe attracts your tribe." This vibe is also written into our numbers and language.

Each number has a specific vibration, including traits and shadows. Having a thorough understanding of 1 through 9 and Master Numbers 11, 22, and 33 is the basis for any Numerological reading.

The shape of numbers and their "flow lines" also reveal vibrational information and meaning. For instance, the number 3 is lucky as it resembles two horseshoes on their sides. The energy of 6 is nurturing as it resembles the belly of a pregnant woman, which represents family. 9 is wise, with the circle at the top forming a head full of wisdom.

You do not have to be psychic, intuitive, or clairvoyant to use Numerology, although improved intuition is one of the positive side effects of learning this ancient science.

Numerology exercises your intuitive muscle, which gets stronger the more you use it. Over time, you will begin to feel the flow lines and vibrations of numbers and receive messages from their shapes and symbolism. You will feel your intuition guiding you and learn to rely on it as you navigate life.

As you start using Numerology, you'll need to separate your imagination and ego from your intuition. The voices in our heads can be so loud that they drown out the intuitive voice within. The more you can keep your ego out of it, the more clearly you will hear the messages of Numerology.

Once you're in the flow and tuning in to vibrations, energy, and your own intuition, Numerology will be so accurate you'll feel like you have a new superpower!

One final word about intuition: remember to use it responsibly. Just because you feel you know something doesn't mean it needs to be vocalized. Use compassion and sensitivity: if it's not kind or it crosses someone's boundaries, it's best left unsaid.

An Inclusive Science

Numerology is applicable to everyone: We all have a name and a birth date to analyze and decipher for hidden aspects of our lives. We all observe numerical patterns as we live our lives. The beauty of Numerology is that you can tap into it no matter your age, location, race, ethnicity, gender expression, ability, or sexuality. It is universal and waiting for you to tap into its power!

All you need is the desire to learn, an awareness of numbers, your own intuition, and a healthy dose of curiosity.

FRIENDS & FAMILY

One of the most exciting aspects of Numerology is learning more about your friends and family. Doing readings for others and seeing how the numbers align with the people close to you will help you better understand their personalities, choices, and behaviors. Being armed with this precious information leads to more successful and fulfilling interactions with those you know—and allows you to analyze your compatibility with those you meet. You will be tuned in to both high and low vibrations as you come across new people, which will allow you to make informed and intuitive decisions about how you let them into your life.

Relationships are our best mirrors, reflecting back our own behaviors and patterns. Doing readings for others can be one of the greatest opportunities for personal awareness, growth, and healing. In families, you made the choice to be reincarnated together, for the purposes of your souls' growth and evolution. Together, your biggest lessons will be highlighted and revealed.

Be forewarned: Once you start sharing your Numerology practice with others, you will likely be met with a mix of skepticism and excitement. Some may feel violated after a reading, become defensive, and insist you are wrong. They may even try to discount the entire field of Numerology. Others will be calling you with the birth dates of online dating profiles, asking for you to make predictions of compatibility. Be sure to take on only what feels right to you. Numerology is a science, but it is also a deep spiritual practice and not one to be taken advantage of. Always protect your intuitive energy!

Tools for Numerology

The only tools you will need for this book are a pen, paper, and someone willing to share their birth date and original birth certificate name.

I've found it works best to do the charts by hand (no calculators) so I can feel the flow lines and shapes of the numbers. This helps me receive intuitive messages. Practice by hand at first. You will eventually find the style and method that works for you.

You'll also need to trust your innate sense of ethics. At the beginning of my Numerology career I struggled with the ethics of revealing too much information about someone who had not given their consent. I always use intuition to guide what information I relay to others—what is relevant and what is better left unsaid. Let your intuition be your guide, your ethical barometer, and a vehicle for compassion. If you do this, your readings will be memorable.

It's time to welcome the myths, math, and magic of Numerology. We'll start by building your personal chart. You'll never see your world in the same way again.

THE SECRETS HIDDEN IN YOUR BIRTHDAY

You came into this world as a soul and without memory of your previous incarnations. With the help of your personal spirit guides, you entered into an agreement I call your *soul contract*. This contract was carefully negotiated to bring you the lessons and experiences your essence craves and to help you achieve maximum growth and soul evolution while here on earth. Your significant relationships, experiences, life events, and circumstances were all chosen specifically for you. This contract contains the specific landing time and date of your birth and dictates a destiny that can be revealed through Numerology.

Within the framework of this contract, there remains free will and personal choice—you can either fulfill your potential or play it small and miss out on your mission. You have the chance to right past wrongs and resolve Karmic relationships, which are relationships with people you have unfinished business with from a past life. (You can spot Karmic Relationships by shared Karmic Debt and Karmic Lessons, see page 14.) Some of us achieve our soul purpose, some take detours, and others have to try again in the next lifetime.

There is much to decipher within your soul contract. We'll start with the secrets your birthday can reveal. Your date of birth reveals two guiding numbers: your Birthday Number and your Life Path Number. As we work through your numerical profile in the following sections, write them down as you go. By the end of chapter 3, you will have all the numbers for your Core Profile.

Let's get started!

Your Birthday Number

In Numerology, we work with the belief that your soul chose the day you were born, giving you the gifts, tools, and lessons you need to fulfill your destiny. The significance of your Birthday Number cannot be overstated. This number provides you with information about who you are, your talents, and your higher purpose. Your Birthday Number comes with a gift, or special talent, that has a big impact on your life.

CALCULATING YOUR BIRTHDAY NUMBER

Your birthday number is the sum of the digits of the day you were born. This is the easiest calculation in Numerology. If your birthday is a single digit (for example, if you were born on the 2nd of the month) then you're done. Your Birthday Number is 2, no reducing necessary. If it's a double digit, like 12, simply add the two numbers together until you reach a single digit. For example:

If your birthday is on the 12th, 1+2=. Your birthday number is 3.

If your birthday is on the 20th, 2+0=. Your birthday number is 2.

If your birthday is on the 28th, 2+8=, 1+0=. Your birthday number is 1.

Adding and reducing to a single digit—called the root number—is where the magic happens in Pythagorean Numerology.

If your birthday is the 11th, 22nd, or 29th (2+9=11) you will not reduce to the single digit. These are Master Numbers and will remain potent the way they are.

Once you have your Birthday Number, write it down in a notebook or on a sheet of paper. We will build your Core Profile from here.

MASTER NUMBERS

Master Numbers are a blessing and a burden. Those born with Master Numbers are given extra gifts and talents, which come with harder lessons and bigger expectations. The obstacles you must overcome are greater than those with birthday numbers of 1 through 9.

For all of the opportunities and possible potential, there is an equal prospective for deceit, duality, and pure evil. History is filled with examples of both from presidents and dictators to famous missionaries and certified super-villains.

From a compatibility perspective, two people with Master Numbers will have an instant understanding of one another on a deep vibrational level.

Karmic Debt

Virtually every chart has karma in it, in the form of either Karmic Debt or Karmic Lessons. Karmic Debt is based on decisions we made in a previous life cycle. The four Karmic Debt numbers are 13, 14, 16, and 19. Karmic Debt can apply to any of the numbers (including Life Path Number, Birthday Number, Destiny Number, Soul Number, or Personality Number—more on those later!) in your profile.

Do You Have Karmic Debt?

You can discover Karmic Debt by looking at the total calculation of a number before reducing. If this number is 13 (reduced to 4), 14 (reduced to 5), 16 (reduced to 7), or 19 (reduced to 1), you have Karmic Debt.

These 4 numbers are always written as fractions to show the total before the reduced single digit:

13/4

14/5

16/7

19/1

If one of these numbers is your prior total, always write the number as a fraction to reveal the debt to be paid. For example, if you were born on the 16th of the month, you know you carry a Karmic Debt of 16/7 in the profile of your Birthday Number.

October 16, 2012, a 10-Month (1+0=1) + 16 + 2012

1 + 16/7 + 5 = 13/4 Life Path Number

This person has both 16/7 and 13/4 Karmic Debt.

10 is also a karmic number, but it does not represent a debt to be paid. It actually indicates that your karma has been paid in full and you are starting with a clean slate!

Meaning of Karmic Debts
The 1 in all Karmic Debt numbers stands for self, meaning you were selfish in a previous life. The second number tells what you were selfish *with*. Here's a quick breakdown:

13/4: The lessons contained in this number carry forward from laziness in a past lifetime. You now need to learn the lessons of hard work, discipline, and overcoming procrastination. Once you prove to the Universe that you are capable of completing something you start, the Universe will stop testing you, and life will become easier. Your hard work and follow-through will be greatly rewarded.

14/5: This debt comes from your overindulgence and abuse of pleasure in a past lifetime. This number rules addictions, so it's very important to avoid addictive substances and behaviors. You may also learn this lesson from a different perspective by deeply loving someone with serious addictions. Your lesson will be moderation.

16/7: This Karmic Debt arises from being irresponsible with love in a past lifetime; it carries the crimes of passion. People with this Karmic Debt often have a hard time communicating and being honest with the ones they love. They tend to be secretive, which can be damaging to relationships and often leads to separation or divorce. The lesson is to overcome jealousy and to be forthright and honest in all communication.

19/1: This number shows up only in very old souls who have epically abused their power in past lives (think corrupt high-ranking military, royal, or political figures). This Karmic Debt leads to trouble with authority figures. It starts with your parents and then carries over to your teachers and eventually your bosses. Simply stated, you do not play well with others. If you can learn to stand up for the underdog or to become a whistle-blower who exposes shady corporate practices, you will be able to resolve this karma.

If you carry Karmic Debt, you *can* fulfill your obligations to the cosmic bank. You will be continually tested and find yourself in the same situations over and over until you learn the lesson and pay your debt.

The Meaning of Your Birthday Number

The vibration of the Birthday Number is one of the easiest to pick up on in someone's energy. This number reveals both a special talent and a lesson. There is some variation in the Birthday Number based on the original number, meaning someone born on the 7th will have a slightly different character than someone born on the 16th or 25th, although there is a common tone to their experiences, talents, and preferences.

BIRTHDAY NUMBER 1

You are independent, competitive, and a natural leader. Full of original ideas, you like to stand out. You take initiative and are able to get people excited. You can also be stubborn, selfish, and moody. Your great lesson is to learn about boundaries, sharing, and teamwork.

BIRTHDAY NUMBER 2

Kind, patient, sensitive, and highly intuitive, you do better in a couple than alone. You are a team player, considerate, and supportive. You do not crave the spotlight. Your lesson is to learn how to stand up for yourself.

BIRTHDAY NUMBER 3

You are friendly and energetic, and your creativity has no limits. You are very social, joyous, and the life of the party. Your lesson is to learn to manage your emotions and to stop seeking instant gratification.

BIRTHDAY NUMBER 4

You are practical, reliable, hardworking, honest, and fair. You are organized and prompt. You like to have a plan and always want to know what to expect. Your lesson is to learn to release control. The 13/4 Karmic Debt will encourage you to contend with procrastination.

BIRTHDAY NUMBER 5

A sense of adventure is your calling card and boredom is your Achilles' heel. Life needs to stay interesting or you check out and move on. You are resourceful, you embrace change, and you can be impulsive. Your lesson is to learn to take responsibility. The 14/5 Karmic Debt will invite you over and over to battle and defeat addictions and overindulgence.

BIRTHDAY NUMBER 6

You are responsible and family-oriented. You also love animals. Loyalty, perfectionism, and thoughtfulness are all part of your nature (although you tend to meddle in affairs that are not yours). You will learn the lessons of surviving betrayal and minding your own business.

BIRTHDAY NUMBER 7

You overanalyze everything, try to find deep meaning in all you do, and are always learning and reading. You love a good conspiracy theory. You are both inquisitive and fiercely private. You need what can seem like an excessive amount of sleep and are curious bordering on meddlesome. Your lesson is to learn to work with others in a selfless way. The 16/7 Karmic Debt will have many lessons to teach you as you dance with love.

BIRTHDAY NUMBER 8

Success is important and attainable for you. You love nice cars, labels, and name-brand anything. Your lesson is to find balance between the spiritual and material and to learn patience and loyalty. You don't always have to learn the hard way.

BIRTHDAY NUMBER 9

You are generous, creative, sensitive, tolerant, and open-minded and take a unique approach to solving problems. You are a humanitarian with a desire to make the world a better place. Be aware of coming across as a know-it-all or condescending. Your lesson is to learn the art of forgiveness and letting go.

MASTER NUMBER 11 (YOUR BIRTHDAY IS THE 11TH OR 29TH)

Your intuitive gifts are abundant. You are kind, and you are a peace-keeper. You're capable of spotting trends and pushing boundaries. You can also be manipulative and capable of extremes. Your lesson is to learn decisiveness and to not give up on your dreams.

MASTER NUMBER 22 (YOUR BIRTHDAY IS THE 22ND)

You are a Master Builder. Many epic firsts have been accomplished by this Birthday Number! You may be the youngest or first to ever accomplish a major milestone. You think outside the box and have true vision. You are powerful and always have the potential of abusing this power. Your lessons will involve your ego.

What About Zero?

You will find zeroes in Birthday Numbers and other numbers in your Core Profile prior to reducing to the root number. Zeroes are important because they are amplifying. The easiest way to understand zero, also called the cipher, is to visualize it holding a mirror up to the number it follows. It will amplify and exaggerate the traits, intensifying its energy.

For example, if you are born on the 20th, the zero will heighten all the traits of the 2, good and bad. Your sensitivity and need to please can be strong. You might even have food allergies or sensitive skin and may find it more difficult to stand up for yourself.

Your Life Path Number

Your Life Path number reveals the special path you will navigate in this lifetime. Life Path is the most important number in your Core Profile, uncovering your natural talents and abilities, character, and unique opportunities and the important lessons that will help you achieve your destiny. It reveals even more about your true nature than any other number. The Life Path provides a blueprint for your opportunities and challenges on this journey.

CALCULATING YOUR LIFE PATH NUMBER

Numerologists use several different methods to calculate the Life Path Number. Some methods are simpler than others, and some can show false Master Numbers and Karmic Debt. To avoid these pitfalls and keep things straightforward, I add each number in the month, day, and year of the birth date individually first. Then I add the 3 reduced digits together.

Month + Day + Year = Life Path Number

In your calculations, use the numerical months of the calendar as follows:

January - 1

February - 2

March - 3

April - 4

May - 5

June - 6

July - 7

August - 8

September - 9

October - 10 (reduces to 1+0=1)

November - 11 (Master Number)

December - 12 (reduces to 1+2=3)

Let's take a look at an example birth date of October 31, 1973.

MONTH: *October is the 10th calendar month (1+0=1), so the month number is 1*

DAY: *31 (3+1 =4), so the Birthday Number is 4*

YEAR: *1973 (1+9+7+3) = 20 (2+0) = 2, so the year number is 2*

Life Path Number is the Month + Day + Year, so in this case it is:

1 + 4 + 2 = 7

Let's try another example that involves Master Numbers: November 29, 1972.

MONTH: *November is the 11ᵗʰ calendar month. 11 is a Master Number, so we don't reduce. The month number is 11.*

DAY: *29 (2+9 =11). 11 is a master number, so we don't reduce. The Birthday Number is 11.*

YEAR: *1972 (1+9+7+2) = 19 (1+9) = 10 (1+0) =1, so the year number is 1.*

The Life Path Number is the Month + Day + Year:

$$11 + 11 + 1 = 23 \ (2+3) = 5$$

Once you've calculated your Life Path Number, write it down under your Birthday Number.

The Meaning of Your Life Path Number

The Life Path Number can show you more information about a person than any other number.

Your Life Path Number reveals where you will find your success, power, and energy. Even more important, it will also uncover the shadow side of your personality and reveal hidden motivations. Once you're tuned in to it, this number can lead you to a fulfilling career that utilizes your natural talents and capabilities as well as nourishing relationships and greater self-awareness. These descriptions also offer insight into the other numbers in your core profile. The placement of each number affects the meaning as well.

ENERGY AND LIFE PATH OF THE 1

You are a born leader, full of original thoughts, inventions, ideas, and vision. Although you are fabulous at getting things started, you're not so great at seeing them through to the end. Tedious details can cause you to lose interest.

In relationships, it's important that you keep your independence, but you also like feeling needed. You like to be in charge—however, you must resist becoming overbearing and selfish.

You come across as capable and confident; however, you struggle with negative self-talk. Remember to take it easy on yourself or you could hinder your ability to progress and achieve your goals.

It is very important that you work to develop self-awareness so you can recognize your lessons and intentionally improve your life and relationships.

When it comes to a career, many 1's are entrepreneurs or bosses— they do not like being told what to do. You are fiercely competitive, which helps you get to the top. Many successful professional athletes and Olympians have this Life Path Number. Without an outlet, this competitive energy can become aggressive and destructive. You must learn to keep your temper in check. Instant gratification and immediate results are what drive you, which can make you impulsive and inconsiderate of others.

The 1 often has health issues related to the digestive system. They can also suffer from migraines, addictions, and stress-related conditions like shoulder and back pain.

The straight line that creates the 1 represents the boundaries you need to develop. It also shows how the 1 stands alone: a unique individual striving for the top.

Famous 1's include Justin Bieber, Tom Cruise, Lady Gaga, David Letterman, Jack Nicholson, and Tiger Woods.

ENERGY AND LIFE PATH OF THE 2

Kindness, diplomacy, and cooperation are all strong traits of the 2. You are the most patient of all the numbers and are extremely sensitive, perceptive, and emotional. Your emotions can switch from crying to laughing on a dime. Along with your sensitivity come true intuitive gifts—you have an innate ability to feel other people's emotions. However, you must be sure not to sacrifice your own opinions and feelings or make compromises simply to keep the peace, as this can breed resentment.

When it comes to relationships, your patient, compromising nature can attract fixer-uppers instead of a mature, suitable mate. You are unlikely to stay single for long and can become a serial dater, moving from one relationship to the next. You are much more comfortable as part of a couple than living on you own.

You're a natural negotiator and mediator. Often the "power behind the throne," you do not always receive the credit or recognition you deserve. You may be overly concerned with what people think. You will find success in careers that allow you to help others—fields like mediation, teaching, or counseling. 2's also have exceptional taste, which they can apply to design work or a career in the arts. 2's can also exercise their strong negotiation skills and intelligence in politics or the law.

The sensitivity of the 2's extends to allergens of all kinds, including food, skin and hair products, dust, chemicals, pharmaceuticals, and many others. Other health issues can include crippling anxiety, depression, and stomach problems.

The shape of the 2 is curvy and compromising, showing that you need to learn how to stand up for yourself.

Famous 2's include Kathy Bates, Angela Bassett, Tony Bennett, Mariah Carey, Jennifer Lopez, and Vera Wang.

ENERGY AND LIFE PATH OF THE 3

3's love the spotlight! You are the life of the party—popular and very social. 3 energy rules expansion. (If you tell a 3 a story, they'll only improve it when they retell it—using exuberance, accents, and definitely some exaggeration.) Your optimism and enthusiasm are infectious. You need an outlet for your creative energy, otherwise it will find an outlet as emotional energy.

Your feelings can be easily hurt, especially with words. This is ironic, since you yourself have a very sharp tongue and rarely struggle with self-expression. In fact, you must watch for becoming sassy, cynical, or moody. Remember that your words can hurt others, so use them carefully. You can be very hard on yourself, and you are often self-deprecating. You use your gift of humor to mask hurt feelings and hide insecurities, but this coping tool may be more transparent than you realize.

In general, your closest relationships need a little more reciprocal action from you. Make sure your people feel appreciated.

The professional gifts of the 3 lie in the creative realm. Musician, actor, artist, dancer, writer, and chef are just a few career options in which you may excel. At a low vibration, you may shrug off responsibility, be disorganized, and indulge in a victim mentality, resentful of anyone who steals the spotlight. When you are vibing high and expressing the positive, you can be an inspirational force, uplifting and bringing joy to those around you.

Health-wise, you have the ability to gain and lose weight quickly, sometimes at an alarming rate. Most 3's are gifted with natural good looks and a beautiful smile. Your fluctuating weight, mental state, and throat issues are health concerns for you to watch out for.

The number 3 looks like a pair of sideways horseshoes and is considered the luckiest number. Never take your good luck for granted!

Famous 3's include Christina Aguilera, Alec Baldwin, David Bowie, Jackie Chan, Katie Couric, Cameron Diaz, Joan Rivers, and Reese Witherspoon.

ENERGY AND LIFE PATH OF THE 4

You are a practical planner who always reads the instructions and is always prepared. You are reliable, dedicated, and prompt. Surprises and change are your kryptonite. You have a desire to control outcomes, so you need to learn how to manage and embrace change and trust life's unseen forces. A pessimist at heart, even on a beautiful day you point out the clouds in the distance and bring your umbrella.

Strong boundaries protect you, but it's important to learn flexibility and accept help from others. Your practical side doesn't always allow you to treat yourself, splurge, or experience the extravagant side of life.

Despite your discipline, procrastination can be a problem for you, especially if you are a 13/4, carrying Karmic Debt (see page 14). These 4's can be quite the opposite of disciplined and want to control every-thing and everyone. At a low vibration, you can be very calculating and manipulative. Be sure to keep your ego in check.

You're naturally friendly but tend not to let others get too close. It is important to show vulnerability in order to develop close rela-tionships. When honesty is your default, others will know you can be trusted.

4's tend to find success in fields like education, business, health care, administration, construction, politics, and accounting. This is the number of the builder. A strong foundation and a nest egg are all you need to feel secure and happy.

Stress-related health issues are common to 4's, including joint pain, migraines, intestinal distress, back problems, obsessive-compulsive disorder, and hypochondria.

4 is made up completely of straight lines, representing the need to maintain order and efficiency. Remember to stay flexible.

Famous 4's include Kate Hudson, Will Smith, Chris Tucker, Bill Gates, and Usher.

ENERGY AND LIFE PATH OF THE 5

Buckle up! The life of the 5 is an exciting and unpredictable ride. Impulsive and always up for anything, you enjoy adventure, freedom, and travel. Rules are more of a suggestion for you, and you tend to bend and disregard them at your will. Boredom can lead you to escapism, which can quickly turn self-destructive. If you are a 14/5, you will struggle with various addictions, both your own and those of the people you love. You are more interested in spending your money on travel and experiences than on material things. You can be a source of concern for your family.

When it comes to relationships, you can be a bit hard to pin down, and you struggle with commitment. You are sensual and require variety and constant stimulation. You *are* capable of commitment and being faithful, it just has to be your idea. You should avoid marrying young, as it will likely end badly.

The talents of the 5 are diverse, and you will be successful in almost anything that holds your interest. You have progressive views and are the first to embrace new ideas. You adapt easily, so technology can be an excellent career choice. You are a natural storyteller and excel at motivating and inspiring others. You can sell absolutely anything with your charm and likability. These traits can lead you to a career in publicity, marketing, working at a start-up, or hairstyling. 5's are often attracted to jobs in uniform, such as security, law enforcement, pilots, or flight attendants. Many are also in hospitality. And there's always self-employment, so nobody can cramp your style or question your vacation days! You also have a natural aptitude for languages.

At a low vibration, you have a tendency to take credit for ideas or work that is not your own. This can damage your reputation and cause people to resent you. Your lessons are in hard work, perseverance, and giving credit where credit is due.

5's are prone to emotional issues, addictions, adrenal burnout, and joint pain. Remember to drink enough water—5's easily become dehydrated.

The shape of the 5 is open on both the right and the left, flat on top, and curvy on the bottom. This gives clues to their need for constant variety and change. Remember to stay grounded.

Famous 5's include Ellen DeGeneres, Mick Jagger, Angelina Jolie, Willie Nelson, Sean Penn, Keith Richards, and Tina Turner.

ENERGY AND LIFE PATH OF THE 6

The 6 vibration is all about LOVE! Charming and charismatic, with a magnetic personality, you have the ability to attract people to whatever cause you have taken up. Generous, kind, and attractive, you are admired and even adored (which completely baffles you). You love to fill your beautiful home with strays—both animals and people. You are truly helpful, not just sympathetic. You are capable of extremes: The 6 has a devil or angel quality.

You are a compassionate individual and make an excellent friend, loyal to the end. Unfortunately, that loyalty is not always reciprocated. One of your lessons will be to understand and experience the true meaning of betrayal, sometimes on an epic scale. You tend to attract the wounded, and you need to be needed—just don't enable those you cannot help. In relationships, you must learn the balance between help and interference.

6's find success in teaching, hospitality, psychology, management, real estate, government, anything relating to animals, or aesthetic fields like fashion, florals, or interior design. You understand life's luxuries better than anyone else. Strong opinions will also get you in trouble. If you find yourself in a constant state of financial stress, you are not living in your purpose. 6's like nice things but are also resourceful. They love a great deal, sometimes too much, as they are also prone to hoarding.

6 has a very strong constitution and a feminine energy. The health issues of 6 will often manifest in the reproductive system and possible cardiac issues.

The shape of the 6 is that of a pregnant woman. One thing is constant for 6: the importance of family. Parents who are 6's find it difficult to view their grown-up children as independent adults and must resist the urge to meddle.

Whether or not you decide to have a family, you will always have wonderful nurturing qualities.

Famous 6's include Victoria Beckham, Bill Maher, Michael Jackson, Stephen King, John Lennon, Richard Nixon, Rosie O'Donnell, and Bruce Willis.

ENERGY AND LIFE PATH OF THE 7

You are smart and mysterious, the strong and silent type. Very analytical, you prefer to do your own research and never take things at face value. If someone has a secret, you (a 7) will find it.

You are skeptical and curious by nature. You are gifted with fabulous intuition; however, spirituality and metaphysics are great mysteries for you. It is important for you, as a 7, to have some type of spiritual or religious beliefs. Without this, your life may lack purpose. Anything with some history or a story of origin interests you. 7's also like to hoard information, often with shelves of unread books. Nature and water are magic for your psyche.

Your knowledge and quick wit give you a unique sense of humor and help you attract admirers. However, intimate relationships can be difficult to maintain, as you appear to be holding back and keeping secrets. Make sure your communication is forthright and honest. (This is especially true if you are a 16/7.) At a low vibration, other lessons will include the experience of being a jealous lover as well as issues of ego. You will learn lessons around maintaining and respecting boundaries and respecting other people's privacy as well as what it is like to have your own boundaries breached.

At a high vibration, you possess a mysterious magnetism and are charming, smart, funny, and attractive. You enjoy making people feel at ease, even though a silent monologue of judgment runs through your mind. A 7 without an outgoing 3 nearby for balance can become reclusive and antisocial.

Fulfilling careers for 7's include researchers, historians, museum curators, criminal profilers, spiritual or religious teachers, or lawyers. You enjoy working alone. Often "a lifer," 7's will work for only a few companies or institutions over their entire career.

Sleep can be elusive for you, and you need all you can get. You are also likely to experience neck problems from holding up that busy head of yours. Meditation, yoga, a bath, or a hike can help you turn off your active mind.

The shape of the 7 resembles a boomerang, which presents itself in relationships, living situations, vacations, and careers. You often find yourself returning to the same people, jobs, and places. The base of the 7 doesn't offer a lot of support. Being out of balance can lead to depression, addictions, and insomnia.

Famous 7's include Muhammad Ali, Christian Bale, Robert Blake, Mel Gibson, Kelsey Grammer, Al Pacino, Jerry Seinfeld, Danielle Steel, and James Woods.

ENERGY AND LIFE PATH OF THE 8

Born to be the boss—if you're not in charge, you'll pretend to be. You're a visionary, but you can also be reckless. Remember, there's a fine line between power and corruption, and you must walk it carefully. You like money and will spend it extravagantly. Anything you do involving money will backfire if done for the wrong reasons. However, success can be yours if you operate with integrity and authenticity. You must remember that rewards may not always be financial—they also come in the form of recognition and legacy. Many 8's experience multiple fortunes and failures in a lifetime.

Showing love and affection is difficult for you. Resist being opinionated and controlling. Your life can be a revolving door of relationships and friendships. At a low vibration, you can have difficulty being loyal and keeping secrets and can come off as hypocritical. Ego, arrogance, and selfishness can be your downfall. Your anger can be explosive, but it always blows over quickly. Learn from these experiences. Take responsibility, sincerely apologize, and evolve.

8's often go through many jobs at different companies, trying to find their niche. As an 8 you will excel at anything in the business world where you can advance and gain influence, such as banking, real estate, finance, and journalism. You're at your best organizing, coaching, supervising, and directing. You are motivated by money, power, and recognition. Work on practicing and improving your tact so your ideas are better received.

Health challenges for 8's include stress-related problems such as high blood pressure and cardiac issues.

The shape of the 8—made up of two conjoined circles—represents the spiritual and material. You must always keep these two worlds in balance. Without balance, the 8 will never find true satisfaction. This symmetrical shape also means that complete and total reversals are possible for you at any time.

Famous 8's include Giorgio Armani, Cindy Crawford, Jane Fonda, Aretha Franklin, Richard Gere, Barbra Streisand, Martin Scorsese, and Elizabeth Taylor.

ENERGY AND LIFE PATH OF THE 9

9's have the energy of an old soul. Many past incarnations have given you lifetimes of subconscious wisdom. Your sense of humor is intelligent and witty. Your laughter is infectious. 9 also has great intuition. You are not impulsive and can think far past instant gratification. Your reasoning is hard to argue with (though it can be tiresome if you're on the wrong side of it). A good student and fast reader, you absorb information like a sponge and will continue to learn throughout your lifetime.

You are charming, magnetic, and romantic and have no trouble attracting a partner. However, it can be challenging to find someone who is as intellectual as you or who can share your sense of humor and really make you laugh.

At a low vibration, you can be condescending. You tend to overexplain things, assuming that others cannot understand. You can also be your own worst enemy, self-sabotaging right when you are on the edge of success or a big payday.

In your career, helping people will feed your soul. You may find fulfillment by inspiring others with your ideas as a writer, artist, or filmmaker. Teaching, counseling, health care professions, and international business are also good options for you. You are also a natural humanitarian and philanthropist who doesn't seek praise or recognition for your good deeds. You are so smart that if you apply your wisdom to criminal activity, you may also be successful at that—though you will ultimately pay the price (if not in this lifetime then the next).

You tend not to express or deal with emotion constructively. This often gets stored in your neck and shoulders, but especially your hips. You must always work on your physical flexibility. Autoimmune conditions may also be a health concern.

The shape of the 9 is a head full of wisdom. You may find that strangers seek you out for random information, advice, or directions.

Famous 9's include Cher, Gandhi, Jack Canfield, Morgan Freeman, Harrison Ford, Shirley MacLaine, Elvis Presley, and Mother Teresa.

Energy and Life Paths of Master Numbers

The Life Paths of Master Numbers have unique and special agreements. These numbers are on a higher plane but are at risk of resting at a lower vibration, squandering a lifetime of opportunity and talent. If you are one of these numbers, you must be careful not to fail at achieving your mission while here on earth.

Master Numbers can be difficult to understand because they essentially oscillate among three distinct vibrations.

For example, the 11 at a lower and easier vibration will take on the traits of the 2, who is cooperative and diplomatic. Sometimes they will exude the energy of an intense double 1, which is more self-involved and arrogant and quite the opposite of the 2. If they reach their potential, they will live in the energy of the 11, a true leader—intuitive, illuminating, and inspiring.

No one can hold their vibration at the highest level indefinitely. It is natural to slip in and out of vibrations, but if you can stay focused, you will ultimately fulfill the destiny of your Master Number.

ENERGY AND LIFE PATH OF MASTER NUMBER 11/2

The Master Number 11 is the most intuitive. You are likely ahead of your time, and the world might not be ready for what you have to offer. Because of this, 11's often don't immediately reap the rewards of their pioneering hard work.

Because of their pioneering spirit, 11/2's make fantastic motivational speakers, spiritual leaders, television hosts, designers, or media personalities.

The 11/2 loves to be in a relationship, especially a peaceful, harmonious one. They will bring their gentle nature and a spiritual quality to any relationship.

Because 11/2's feel things so deeply, this can lead to depression, anxiety, and serious allergies. The unique vibration of the 11 makes you prone to the health issues of both the 1 and the 2.

Famous 11/2's include Jennifer Aniston, Coco Chanel, Bill Clinton, Harry Houdini, Prince Charles and Prince William, Barack and Michelle Obama, Ronald Reagan, and Tony Robbins.

ENERGY AND LIFE PATH OF MASTER NUMBER 22/4

The Master Number 22/4 is known as the Master Builder. The 22 is uniquely gifted with the ability to turn vision into reality. Creating an empire and leaving a legacy are of great importance to them.

Because the 22 is a double dose of 2 energy, they live with a nervous tension they must learn to channel into their visionary plans. A 22/4 will face tests of ethical conduct and responsibility. Their family of origin tends to be complex.

The 22 will look for a high-achieving partner who makes them feel secure. They are attracted to partners who are practical and goal-oriented.

Learning to believe in others, rather than trying to control or manipulate them, is a lesson for 22's. Share your vision and let people contribute. You need them more than you think.

The 22 is capable of extremes and has the potential to use their powers for either good or evil. Your greatest rewards will come from humanitarian and well-intended endeavors.

This number loves to put their name on things, and I'm not just talking about a monogram.

The unique vibration of the 22 means you are prone to both the allergies and stress issues of 4 and 2.

Famous people with 22/4 Life Paths include Sir Richard Branson, Tina Fey, Chris Hemsworth, the 14th Dalai Lama, Sir Paul McCartney, and Caroline Myss.

ENERGY AND LIFE PATH OF MASTER NUMBER 33/6

The 33/6 is known as the Master Teacher. They are the most influential and compassionate of the Master Numbers.

33/6, you are highly knowledgeable and thoroughly research all of your ideas before sharing them. At your highest potential, your communication is clear, without any personal agenda, and you have a genuine concern for humanity.

To be a true 33/6, the calculation must include either an 11 or 22 Master Number. (Otherwise, if you have a 33 double digit as your Life Path Number, it is ultimately reduced to the root number 6 and does not have the "Master" designation).

In a relationship, you need to focus on mastering your emotions. Magnetic and attractive, you never have a problem finding a partner. However, be careful of taking on complicated personalities that are needy yet unwilling to help themselves.

33's love helping and healing. Fulfillment comes from helping others and sharing your wisdom and artistic gifts with the world. Career paths include any that support human rights, education, health care, and artists of all mediums. Remember to practice self-care.

The unique vibration of the 33 means you are prone to the health issues of the 6 and the 3: both reproductive and cardiac issues as well as depression and fluctuations in weight.

Many Hollywood stars benefit from the creative and emotional double dose of 3 energy. Meryl Streep is one of the rare, true 33/6's, born June 22, 1949 (6+**22**+5=**33/6**). Senator Elizabeth Warren shares this same birth date. Film director Francis Ford Coppola is also a true 33/6; he was, born April 7, 1939 (4+7+**22**=**33/6**).

33 is more commonly found in a Destiny Number where the Soul or Personality Numbers are an 11 and 22, or vice versa (more on this in chapter 3).

Putting It All Together: Birthday and Life Path Numbers

Combining a person's Birthday Number with their Life Path Number reveals synergistic and complex character traits. Learning these and paying attention to the number profile as a whole will bring more accuracy to your readings.

For example, if someone has a Life Path Number of 9 and a Birthday Number of 8, they may struggle with generosity. The 9 energy wants to leave a big tip for their server, but the character of the 8 instantly regrets it.

Finding both a 3 and a 7 in the Core Profile is one of the most common patterns. These numbers provide a sort of balance for one another, even though they are internally at odds. A 7 Life Path needs time alone and can be reclusive while a 3 Birthday loves the spotlight, likes to talk, and is very social. This causes an internal contradiction that the person must constantly navigate.

Some combinations are trickier. For instance, a Life Path 6 with a prominent 1 will have a tendency to exaggerate and fabricate, casting responsibility aside in favor of selfish endeavors. Richard Nixon comes to mind. The strong opinions of the 6 combined with the stubborn nature and competitiveness of the 1 can be a volatile cocktail. When a Birthday Number and Life Path Number are not in harmony, it can cause indecisiveness, contradicting purposes, and a lot of second-guessing. It also creates a dynamic and interesting approach to life. People may have a hard time figuring you out because your actions can be led by either your Life Path or your Birthday energy.

Understanding the strengths and weaknesses of the numbers in your profile will empower you as you decode your unique gifts. When your numbers are different, they also provide extra resources that can help you identify and overcome challenges. Overall, your birth date numbers give you the strongest and most accurate information about your character.

In the next chapter, you'll learn to decode the power and secrets of your name, revealing so much about your true nature, including your Destiny Number, Soul Number, Personality Number, and Maturity Number. More and more will be revealed as you examine the numerical value of your name and continue to build your Core Number Profile.

3

THE SECRETS HIDDEN IN YOUR NAME

The name given to you at birth was chosen in a moment of intuition and divine inspiration by those who named you. Your birth name gives you the vibrational energy you need on your life journey. In this chapter, you will learn how to assign numerical energy to letters in order to understand the significance of your birth name and uncover your Destiny, Soul, Personality, and Maturity Numbers.

Your Birth Name

In Numerology, it is of utmost importance to use the full name on your original birth certificate. This is true even if you don't like your name, had it for only a few minutes, have changed the spelling, changed your last name for marriage or other reasons, or even changed your entire name. This original name is your Destiny. Its numerical value is known as your Destiny Number, and its meaning is powerful.

If you do not know your original name (for instance, if you were given a new name at adoption), you may then use the one you know—you have grown into this name.

Your birth name includes your middle name(s) and excludes any suffixes like Jr., the 3rd or III, and hyphens.

Your Destiny Number

Your Destiny Number reveals your mental and physical talents as well as the shadows in your character. The Destiny Number represents the highest potential that you will spend a lifetime trying to reach and fulfill. It is the expression of your goals relating to career, family, and the type of person you want to be.

CALCULATING YOUR DESTINY NUMBER

To discover your Destiny Number, write out your full name in all capitals. Under each letter, write the correlated numerical value from the chart on page 41.

As we did with the month, day, and year of your Life Path Number, we will first add up the numbers in each name separately and then reduce to a single digit. That's it! You can add your Destiny Number to your profile.

Let's use Elvis Presley as our first example.

Letter Number Calculator

Each letter of the alphabet has a numerical value that correlates to its placement in the alphabet.

For example: M is the 13th letter (1+3=4) so reduces to 4, J is the 10th letter so reduces 1, T the 20th letter and reduces to 2, and so on. Over time, you'll know these values by heart but for now, you can refer to this chart for your readings.

LETTERS & THEIR NUMBERS

1	2	3	4	5	6	7	8	9
A	B	C	D	E	F	G	H	I
J	K	L	M	N	O	P	Q	R
S	T	U	V	W	X	Y	Z	

ELVIS AARON PRESLEY

5 3 4 9 1   1 1 9 6 5   7 9 5 1 3 5 7

Elvis $5+3+4+9+1 = 22/4$

Aaron $1+1+9+6+5 = 22/4$

Presley $7+9+5+1+3+5+7 = 37\ (3+7=10)\ 1+0 = 1$

$22/4 + 22/4 + 1 = 45\ (4+5 = 9)\ 9$

Elvis has a Destiny Number of 9.

Now, let's try Stevie Nicks (remember we must use her given name of Stephanie):

S T E P H A N I E   L Y N N   N I C K S

1 2 5 7 8 1 5 9 5   3 7 5 5   5 9 3 2 1

Stephanie $1+2+5+7+8+1+5+9+5 = 43\ (4+3) = 7$

Lynn $3+7+5+5 = 20\ (2+0) = 2$

Nicks $5+9+3+2+1 = (2+0) = 2$

$7 + 2 + 2 = 11/2$

Stevie Nicks has a Destiny Number of 11/2.

Lady Gaga was born as:

S T E F A N I   J O A N N E

1 2 5 6 1 5 9   1 6 1 5 5 5

A N G E L I N A   G E R M A N O T T A

1 5 7 5 3 9 5 1   7 5 9 4 1 5 6 2 2 1

Stefani $1+2+5+6+1+5+9 = 29\ (2+9) = 11/2$

Joanne $1+6+1+5+5+5 = 23\ (2+3) = 5$

Angelina $1+5+7+5+3+9+5+1 = 36\ (3+6) = 9$

Germanotta $7+5+9+4+1+5+6+2+2+1 = 42\ (4+2) = 6$

$11+5+9+6 = 31\ (3+1) = 4$

Lady Gaga has a Destiny Number of 4.

The Meaning of Your Destiny Number

Now that you know how to calculate this highly important number, let's dive into the meaning of each Destiny Number and what they reveal about the nuanced layers of personality, natural talents, and career and the shadow side of one's character.

DESTINY NUMBER 1: THE LEADER AND DECISION MAKER

You like to get your own way—and usually do. Your career must have room for upward mobility in order for you to stay motivated, and you will likely end up in charge.

Your inventive mind gives you quick problem-solving skills.

You have great vision and innovative ideas and excel at getting people on board to bring your ideas into reality. 1's get excited about ideas—really excited—but can lose interest when it comes to the details and often struggle with follow-through. Remember to set boundaries and to stand up for yourself.

You fear failure. If you don't think you'll be the best at something, you won't even try. When living from your shadow side, you can be bossy, impatient, arrogant, and selfish and use your influence for evil.

Embrace your leadership gifts of inspiration, independent thinking, and unique ideas. Your originality should to be shared. Ultimately the Destiny Number 1 will demand you utilize these gifts and create opportunities to fulfill your vision.

DESTINY NUMBER 2: THE TEAM PLAYER

Destiny Number 2 is naturally tactful, charming, good with details, cooperative, and patient. You excel as part of a team and are better in a partnership than a leadership position.

You tend to second-guess yourself and lack confidence in your choices. The sensitivity that allows you to work so well with others can be a delicate balance in the workplace. Since you don't like to be the center of attention, you must make sure that others recognize and appreciate your efforts and give you credit where credit is due, or you may be overlooked. People trust you and admire your thoughtful, generous nature. If you don't feel this respect from others, you will not be comfortable or perform well.

When living from your shadow side, you become overly sensitive, a crybaby, sneaky, manipulative, and a convincing liar, revealing your duality. You can become confrontational instead of diplomatic.

You will be happiest when you are making a positive and dynamic contribution to a team. Bring harmony, balance, and cooperation to everything you do, and you will feel fulfilled and overcome your shadow. Whether it is with family, friends, or colleagues, become a peacemaker and a harmonizing influence in whatever situation you find yourself.

DESTINY NUMBER 3: THE ARTIST AND ENTERTAINER

While uber-creative, Destiny Number 3 may suffer from Peter Pan syndrome and never want to grow up. You have a terrific sense of humor and like your work to feel fun and uplifting. This is all well and good, but you must also take your responsibilities seriously. What others recognize and encourage as your natural talents may not be the ones that bring you joy. It's important to strive for balance. In addition to fun, you experience all emotions on an intense level. Try to temper your sensitivity and not take things so personally.

Others may feel you have a charmed life and feel envious of how things always work out for you. On the flip side, you feel jealous of anyone you perceive to be stealing your thunder or who seems to be more talented, popular, or gifted than you. Remember, there's plenty of success to go around.

On the shadow side, a 3 must avoid being overly dramatic or emotional, deceitful, intolerant, and jealous. Keep these childish feelings in check and you will experience more of the joy you're seeking.

DESTINY NUMBER 4: THE PLANNER AND PRODUCER

You are reliable, dependable, organized, and on time. You may resent people who aren't like this, but you also have the skills to manage them. You have an amazing ability to stay calm in the face of chaos and bring order to everything you do.

Practical achievements bring you great satisfaction, like paying off your car or having a clean house. However, control is an illusion, and you must learn to relinquish it.

You're always the one with the plan, but others are often oblivious to all the hard work you've put in. You are able to break down tasks into bite-size pieces and steadily make progress, although secretly you would love someone to take things off your plate.

On the shady side, you can be a workaholic, opinionated, antagonistic, and moody. Resentment can make you downright cruel. Learning to delegate, bring visibility to your work, and take more time for fun is important for you. If you have a Karmic Debt of 13/4, your struggle to complete things will be a major life theme.

DESTINY NUMBER 5: THE THRILL-SEEKING PROGRESSIVE

You always have a story to tell, a place to be, a trip to take, and people to see. Others admire your adventurous spirit and like to live vicariously through you. You must remember not to take things too far and that life can be exciting without being destructive.

To feel fulfilled in your career, you will need a lot of variety, so office life may not be right for you. Your charismatic personality and gift of gab make you a natural at sales, marketing, or promotion.

You can get caught up in drama or gossip, sometimes creating or fabricating a scenario in order to entertain yourself. Since you get bored easily, you may find yourself surrounded by people who are always in crisis. To avoid this situation, which will drain your impressive energy, work at gaining a deeper understanding of yourself and others.

Your shadow side can cause you to be impulsive, restless, outspoken, rude, and even profane. Your downfall can be the crazy choices you make without giving thought to consequence. Beware of your self-destructive tendencies.

DESTINY NUMBER 6: THE NURTURING PERFECTIONIST

One of your best qualities is your loyalty although, sadly, it is rarely returned. You've likely been shaped by having family responsibilities from a young age. Having a happy and stable home is important to you, and you excel in the realms of the domestic. You make a wonderful parent, and if you don't have children, you will channel your nurturing nature into animals.

You are sensible, mature, and trustworthy. Responsibility feeds your soul. You are a good judge of character and give great advice, playing the role of counselor to your friends (and possibly professionally as well). You want to beautify your surroundings: Pretty things bring you joy and comfort.

Your shadow is that you can be smug, sarcastic, and conceited, believing no one can do the job as well as you. Others may mistake your high personal standards as competition or condescension. You tend to meddle, worry, and seek constant recognition. Don't get too caught up in what other people think or in other people's problems.

DESTINY NUMBER 7: THE INTELLECTUAL INTUITIVE

You radiate a quiet dignity. You think very deeply about things, and your daydreams may result in philosophical or technological genius. You are poised, reserved, observant, refined, and spiritual. You can be alone and not lonely, which is difficult for many other Destiny Numbers. Nature and solitude work well for you.

Your intuition is so strong that sometimes you can "see" other people's thoughts. Your dreams are prophetic. You possess a great memory and are interested in history, collections, and the past. You'll excel in a field where you can specialize or become a true expert.

7's often grew up feeling like their parents were keeping secrets from them. Even if this was for your protection, it created and nurtured a very real paranoia within you. You are a keeper of secrets and tend to be a bit of a loner. You work diligently, sometimes for years, toward your goals in life and work.

Your shadow will bring out suspicion, dishonesty, paranoia, sneakiness, and jealousy. A strong sense of spirituality, whatever that may personally look like for you, will ground you, provide balance, and bring out your best. You will be either very scientific or very spiritual, but there are some who can strike a balance between the two. Cultivate at least a few close relationships. It's important to share your vast wisdom and knowledge with the world.

DESTINY NUMBER 8: THE EXECUTIVE

You are made to succeed and be financially flush. You learned about power and status early in life and need to be an authority in your chosen profession in order to feel fulfilled. Luckily, you are a natural leader and influencer.

You love achievement but need to watch out—you may never be satisfied, always wanting to do more, be more, have more. You tend to value the material, but a legacy of kindness and generosity is far more memorable.

Failure is devastating to you, but not trying is worse, so you will need to be daring in the face of your fears. Over time, you'll realize that people respond to who you are, not what you do or what you have.

The shadow side of the 8 can breed impatience, intolerance, ruthlessness, and sometimes a violent temper. You can abuse substances and experience financial problems. You must always seek balance. Your desires will be fulfilled when you bring a spiritual grounding into your material world.

DESTINY NUMBER 9: THE WISE HUMANITARIAN

You can win almost anyone over with your sense of humor, outgoing personality, and charm. You are a visionary and will inspire others to join a movement that will make the world a better place. You can be idealistic and even naive about other people's motives. You are impressionable and prone to forming habits, which can include substance abuse.

You are patient, charitable, compassionate, and romantic. You want the world's approval and secretly seek fame. Sharing your unique gifts, helping humanity, teaching, advising, and healing all feed your soul. While you are saving the world, make sure you don't neglect those closest to you.

Your shadow side can be possessive, moody, shy, naive, and restless. A shopaholic, you can squander money.

MASTER NUMBER 11: THE MASTER INTUITIVE

This number has a potent expression. Extremely sensitive, intuitive, and aware, you exude a powerful, refined, and elegant presence. You experience divine guidance, and your natural leadership abilities mean you can easily attract a following or fame.

You make decisions using an elusive combination of logic, intuition, and emotion. You've always known you are different and with time will fully embrace your special gifts to awaken and enlighten others.

When living in your shadow, you can be manipulative and use your power for morally questionable endeavors. You can have a hard time separating your imagination from reality. You often feel like no one can live up to your high expectations.

MASTER NUMBER 22: THE MASTER ARCHITECT

You've been aware of the bigger picture from a young age, and you always dream big. You have the most potential for success of any Destiny Number and want to leave a real mark on the world. You will be able to harness your massive gifts as an adult, once you really begin to understand what you are capable of. You will achieve big things.

From your shadow side, you can be sly and underhanded in business, destructive, and even evil. You must always use your powers for good.

MASTER NUMBER 33: THE MASTER INFLUENCER

To be a true Destiny Number 33/6, you must have a Soul Number (see page 51) of 11 or 22 or a Personality Number (see page 53) of 11 or 22.

A Destiny Number 33 is a massive mission to fulfill, but you're all about responsibility, so you're ready for the challenge.

You have outstanding creative abilities, communication, sincerity, and compassion. Service to others will reveal spiritual gifts for you. Kind and unpretentious, you give with no expectation of return. You are a visionary who is full of joy, fun, and compassion, and you easily make heartfelt connections.

You are the Master Influencer. It is your destiny to be an example of the true power of love and compassion for the world. You are a helper and a healer.

The shadow side of the 33 is martyrdom—and you can be whiny. You often take on the pain or scars of others. You will find great rewards when you use your natural healing gifts to help others and provide the tools for people to help themselves.

Choosing Baby Names

If you're thinking of becoming a parent, one of your first big responsibilities is choosing a name. Your choice will shape the destiny of another soul and the fate of your child's life!

Be sure to tap into your intuition when picking a name. For many parents, the name comes in a dream or a moment of divine inspiration. If a name doesn't feel quite right, then don't settle! You will know deep in your soul when the right name has come to you.

Trying to select or give your child what you perceive as power numbers or a profile that will make them, for example, a star athlete is not advised. Use Numerology to bring awareness to your decision: choose numbers that can help the child avoid painful karma, or try to provide balance, or are in harmony with your own numbers, but not to attempt to build some ideal personality. You have only so much control. The baby will choose their birth date (even if the birth is scheduled), so their intended lessons will come via their Birthday and Life Path Numbers regardless of the birth name. If the soul needs the lesson of addiction, they will choose to be born on the 14th of the month, or if they want lessons about power and authority figures, they will choose the 19th or a date that adds up to a Life Path 19/1.

I've also had the exciting experience of working with clients who were twins, sharing the same Life Path and Birthday Number. Because of their very different Soul, Personality, and Destiny Numbers, they lived out very different lives and experiences. This shows how important your name is.

Some Numerologists don't believe in assisting in name choice. This does not resonate with me, and I am happy to provide support and guidance, knowing that the client/parent always has the ultimate intuition and choice. But why not take advantage of the tools you have? Numerology can reveal possible imbalances and special harmonies between parent and child and reduce excessive Karmic Debt and Karmic Lessons.

If you don't consult a Numerologist before birth, examining your child's Core Profile after they are born is still an asset. It will help you get to know this new soul, better nurture their gifts, and more deeply understand their lessons.

The Universe is much more magical than we give it credit for, always guiding us and working with our plans. Numerology can lift the veil of this powerful hidden force.

Your Soul Number

This is the number that rules decisions made by the heart. Sometimes called the Heart's Desire Number, it reveals your private self that only those closest to you get to see. It's where your dreams, desires, longings, and true inner motivations lie and dictates how you operate in heartfelt relationships.

When this number is in harmony with your Life Path Number, you will make decisions easily. When it is the same as your Life Path Number, you will wear your heart on your sleeve. Your private self will read more like an open book. If your Soul Number and Life Path Number are in conflict, you will be indecisive—your head and your heart will want different things. If this is the case, you will be a little more complex and surprise people with your actions or decisions at times.

Your Soul Number is the total sum of all the **vowels** in your full birth certificate name. Write the letters in all caps and their corresponding numerical values from the chart on page 41. Then add and reduce to arrive at your Soul Number. Let's stick with Elvis as an example.

5		9			1	1		6				5			5	
E	L	V	I	S	A	A	R	O	N	P	R	E	S	L	E	Y
	3	4		1			9		5	7	9		1	3		7

VOWELS

Elvis   5+9 = **14 (1+4) = 14/5**

Aaron   1+1+6 = **8**

Presley 5+5 = **10 (1+0) = 1**

5 + 8 + 1 = **14/5 (1+4) 5**

Elvis has a Soul Number of 14/5 (write as a fraction to note the Karmic Debt).

What to Do With "Y"

So, is "y" a vowel or not? I'm sure you're not here for a phonics lesson, but this is important! Getting it wrong can affect your entire profile.

The easiest way to determine if the "y" in your name is a vowel or consonant is whether or not it is next to another vowel. Having vowels on either side of a "y" will likely make the "y" a consonant. For example, the "y" in Murray, Yolanda, or Presley are consonants.

A consonant next to a "y" will likely make the "y" a vowel, as found in the name Kyle, Pythagoras, Mary, or Lynn. I say "likely" because there is—of course—an exception to this rule.

If the "y" *sounds* like a vowel, even when placed next to a vowel, then it will also be a vowel. For example, the names Wyatt, Bryan, or Kyara. In all these instances the "y" is responsible for a vowel sound, so it functions as a vowel.

Your Personality Number

This is the number that dictates the first impression you make on others. Knowing your Personality Number will give you a better understanding of how others perceive you.

The Personality Number is expressed in the external image you choose to project through your reactions, behaviors, and responses, whether consciously or unconsciously.

The Personality Number is a gatekeeper to your true nature. It is there to protect your feelings and heart. It censors what you send out and what kind of people or information you let in. It acts as a filter for who and what gets to enter your inner world, deflecting certain vibrations and choosing those that best resonate with you.

The Personality Number is also a career directive, as it projects your natural talent and ability. It is the number that usually gets you hired.

Your Personality Number is the total sum of all the **consonants** in your full birth certificate name.

Elvis   3+4+1 = **8**

Aaron   9+5 = **14 (1+4) = 14/5**

Presley   7+9+1+3+7 = **27 (2+7) = 9**

                8 + 5 + 9 = **22/4**

Elvis has a Personality Number of 22/4.

Add your Soul Number and Personality Number to your Core Profile.

TIP: *To check your math and make sure you haven't made an error, you can follow this pro shortcut: Your Soul + Personality Number = Your Destiny Number.*

Meanings of Soul and Personality Numbers

The general energy of the numbers 1 to 9, 11, 22, and 33 always remain the same—whether they show up in your Birthday Number, Life Path Number, Destiny Number, or elsewhere. The placement and combination of the numbers is where they get their nuanced meaning.

SOUL NUMBER 1: THE CHARMER

With unique style and image, this take-charge number will be the leader in a relationship. You tend to build walls of protection and can have a damaging "I'll hurt you before you can hurt me" mentality. Deep down, you are a hopeless romantic.

Your charm will take you far, but you expect to find that same trait in your mate and want others to be as clever and independent as you are. You inspire innovation and don't participate in mediocrity.

SOUL NUMBERS 2 & 11: THE DEVOTED

Better in a pair than alone, you won't find Soul Number 2 single for long. They will be committed and expect the same from their partner—definitely the marrying kind.

The 2 is likely to do whatever it takes to keep the peace. You are tactful and kind, can see both sides of a situation, and prefer to be the support in a relationship rather than take the lead.

Since they are extremely sensitive, criticism can be beyond hurtful to 2's. As a 2, you are extremely giving, and it is of utmost importance that you feel appreciated.

As an 11/2 Soul Number, the emotional highs and lows will be intense. The double 1's can cause selfishness. Make sure you are using your powers of persuasion for a worthy cause, not for manipulation and personal gain.

You bring a deep spiritual quality to any relationship.

SOUL NUMBER 3: THE FLIRT

Enchanting and flirty, the Soul Number 3 makes others laugh and feel special with their sparkling personality. You tend to follow the fun and struggle with a "grass is always greener" mentality, which can cause you to be noncommittal in relationships.

You may hide your true emotions with humor and excessive talking. If you are not happy, others will know from your words, which can be like knives, intended to hurt.

Your lesson is to always give others the recognition they deserve, to not take people for granted, and to not make them feel like your sidekick.

SOUL NUMBERS 4 & 22: THE STRAIGHT SHOOTER

The Soul Number 4 can appear cold or aloof. Emotions can be volatile, and the 4 likes to keep them under control along with everything else. This number takes a practical approach to everything, including love, and may not seem very romantic on the surface.

You are capable of romance, but that romantic gesture or dinner will be planned and executed perfectly. You prefer giving and receiving practical rather than whimsical gifts.

Your best quality is that you are dependable and will build a well-ordered life, offering strong support to your partner. You'll want to find a stable love with someone you trust to help you build your dreams.

As a 22/4, you will have the desire to leave a legacy. To fulfill this mission, you will need to commit every ounce of yourself to it.

SOUL NUMBER 5: THE FREE SPIRIT

Freedom is essential to the happiness of the 5. With a deep passion for change, travel, and adventure, you need to feel unrestricted in your relationships. Promises can be hard to keep, and 5's do not respond well to ultimatums.

Since 5's are ruled by the senses, sex is especially important to this number. The 5 always wants variety, and that extends to the bedroom. Sensory pleasures bring you happiness but can also lead to overindulgence and abuse.

This number tends to get married later in life. Soul Number 5's resist emotional attachments and lasting commitments.

SOUL NUMBERS 6 & 33: THE LOVER

The biggest desire of the Soul Number 6 is to love and be loved in return. Sentimental, patient, compassionate, and understanding, you make a great partner and make love uncomplicated.

6's tend to idealize love, create an image of a beautiful and perfect life, and then strive for it. Soul Number 6 will expect commitment. The 6 needs to be needed, and you enjoy listening and giving advice and support.

With a deep love of their home and family, 6's generally choose to have children of their own—although, of course, not always.

The 33/6 wants to raise the world's love vibration. You're emotional and want to bring understanding to the world through love.

SOUL NUMBER 7: THE MYSTERIOUS ONE

Your intelligence makes you charming and refined. You give others the impression that you prefer to keep things private.

This Soul Number may choose a life of solitude, preferring your own company to that of others. If you do couple up, it will be when you are mature and within a very private and safe relationship. You may find the idea of becoming a monk or nun appealing.

You prefer to talk about facts rather than unpredictable feelings and emotions. Your impersonal approach to romantic relationships can cause distrust, as the other person might feel that you are with-holding from them. Becoming emotionally vulnerable and making deep connections is out of your comfort zone but necessary for a ful-filling life.

SOUL NUMBER 8: THE STRIVER

8's like to learn the hard way, and matters of the heart are no excep-tion. You may find yourself in relationships with the same types of people over and over again. This can be emotionally and financially draining. Recognize your romantic pattern and stop chasing your tail.

This number enjoys material comforts and wealth. It is important for you that others perceive you as successful. You dream big and are not afraid of hard work. You need to be challenged (and rewarded for rising to the challenge), even within relationships, or you will slip to the low vibration, becoming sadistic, cruel, depressed, and frustrated.

Your ideal partner needs to be attractive, capable, and as driven as you are.

Whether intentional or not, this number tends to marry well or partner with someone with resources who can support their vision and need for material success.

Remember there is no room for hypocrisy in love—treat your part-ner as you would like to be treated.

SOUL NUMBER 9: THE BIGHEARTED ONE

This number wants Universal Love and is genuinely concerned for the well-being of humankind. As old souls, Soul Number 9's are wise and gifted with exceptional intuition.

This number is thoughtful and will always anticipate the needs of their partner, often treating them like a king or queen. In a relationship with a 9 you will often find a significant age difference.

You secretly dream of having a big impact on the world and maybe even fame, although you possess a charming humility. Perceptive and generous, you are often torn between your own needs and the needs of others.

Emotional and sensitive, you can also be critical and moody. You'll be frustrated when people can't meet your high expectations or help themselves in the face of opportunity.

PERSONALITY NUMBER 1: DYNAMIC & EFFICIENT

Stylish, cheerful, controlled, capable, dominant, aggressive, unreceptive, intimidating, courageous.

PERSONALITY NUMBERS 2 & 11: FRIENDLY & UNPRETENTIOUS

Cooperative, modest, diplomatic, humble, a good listener, shy, refined, often underestimated.

PERSONALITY NUMBER 3: INSPIRING & CHARMING

Attractive, uplifting, magnetic, extroverted, optimistic, chatty, fun, affectionate, scattered, flippant.

PERSONALITY NUMBERS 4 & 22: RELIABLE & CONSISTENT

Practical appearance, respectable, conservative, reliable, trustworthy, responsible, reserved, inflexible, egotistical.

PERSONALITY NUMBER 5: SPARKLING & WITTY

Upbeat, progressive, optimistic, up for anything, sexually attractive, outgoing, exuberant, magnetic, youthful appearance, irresponsible.

PERSONALITY NUMBERS 6 & 33: UNDERSTANDING & COMPASSIONATE

Protective, reliable, resourceful, domestic, elegant, perfectionist, sympathetic, capable, nurturing, tasteful.

PERSONALITY NUMBER 7: SERIOUS & MYSTERIOUS

Perceptive, observant, intelligent, dignified, reserved, introspective, introverted, philosophical, private, eccentric, aloof.

PERSONALITY NUMBER 8: STRONG & IMPRESSIVE

Influential, powerful, ambitious, authoritative, business-minded, visionary, confident, refined, ruthless, greedy, conceited, controlling.

PERSONALITY NUMBER 9: IMPRESSIVE & CHARISMATIC

Competent, determined, honest, stable, creative, masterful, efficient, diplomatic, arrogant, intimidating, envy-inducing.

Karmic Lessons

Karmic Lessons are revealed by the missing energy in your name, represented by missing letters. There are nine possible Karmic Lessons, although most people have only two or three.

Think of the missing energy as tools that you can't easily access. You must instead learn to develop these skills on your own.

Here is a breakdown of the meaning of the missing letters in your name:

Lesson 1: missing A, J, and S
You will learn how to stand up for yourself and promote yourself. Your lesson is independence and taking initiative.

Lesson 2: missing B, K, and T
You will learn patience, cooperation, and to be more tactful and diplomatic. Your Karmic Lesson will be to learn sensitivity toward other people's feelings and to play well on a team.

Lesson 3: missing C, L, and U
This lesson will teach the value of self-love and how to not be too serious or self-critical. You will be tested in areas of communication and imagination and learn to practice joy and optimism.

Lesson 4: missing D, M, and V
If you are missing Lesson 4, you will struggle to stay organized. You need to build a foundation and learn discipline in order to avoid scattering your energies. Procrastination is often an issue.

Lesson 5: missing E, N, and W

You will learn to embrace change and new experiences. Your lesson is to find some adventure in your life and overcome your fears by having faith in the Universal plan.

Lesson 6: missing F, O, and X

You face major commitment issues and have difficulty showing emotion. You dodge responsibility and must work to establish sincere, vulnerable relationships. There may be family scars that require resolution or forgiveness.

Lesson 7: missing G, P, and Y

You must learn the lesson of authenticity and seek spiritual enlightenment. You may struggle with learning and school. Stick with it in order to specialize and perfect your talents.

Lesson 8: missing H, Q, and Z

Your lesson is in managing money—both through an abundance and a lack of wealth. You will learn how to handle your resources, better tolerate authority figures, and accept the advice of others.

Lesson 9: missing I and R

You lack humanitarianism and will learn to be more compassionate, understanding, and tolerant. You will be forced to sacrifice a personal ambition for the good of all. You will learn the importance of community and forgiveness.

The effect of any of the Karmic Lessons will be diminished and easier if you have the missing number included somewhere else in your Core Profile. Be sure to add any Karmic Lessons to your profile now so you can remain aware of them.

The Concords

In Numerology, there are three unique concords (sometimes called triads) of numbers that naturally go together. These are:

1, 5, and 7

2, 4, and 8

3, 6, and 9

Within each group, the numbers share common interests and traits. On a very basic level, these concords can be used to predict how well you will get along with other numbers and the likelihood of a long relationship or friendship with someone you meet.

To identify your personal concord, find the group that contains your reduced Birthday Number or Life Path Number. You'll probably find that many of your friends, romantic relationships, and people you share common interests with will be part of your concord. With these people, you will find a natural understanding and bond.

If your Birthday and Life Path fall into different concords, you may find that you don't always know what you want. When you meet people for the first time, consider both concords and pay attention to how you relate to them on different levels. Check for your numbers in the concords that follow.

1-5-7: THE MENTAL CONCORD

These are the intellects—the curious, scientific, analytical, and technological. They will participate in endless learning throughout their lives and generally approach things from a rational rather than emotional perspective.

2-4-8: THE BUSINESS-MINDED CONCORD

These numbers are where the moneymakers, workaholics, and corporate ladder climbers are found. They are career-minded achievers and find success in business development, operations, and management. They are generally practical, grounded, and efficient.

3-6-9: THE CREATIVE CONCORD

Artistic, spiritual, and inspiring, those in this triad are expressive and live from the heart. They have a strong interest in and understanding of the metaphysical and spiritual and tend to be creative and emotional.

The Maturity Number

You will not feel The Maturity Number strongly until you reach your 40s, and it won't be actualized until you are around age 50. This number is where your true self is found and can help you finally feel comfortable in your own skin. This number plays an important role as you grow older, integrating with your Life Path Number and providing a theme for the second half of your human experience.

If your Maturity Number is part of a concord with your other numbers, the shift in your energy will be subtle. If it is a brand-new number, the changes will be dramatic.

Your Maturity Number

To find your Maturity Number, simply add your Life Path and Destiny Numbers.

Life Path + Destiny Number = Maturity Number

Example: 7 Life Path + 1 Destiny Number = 8 Maturity Number

7 and 1 both belong to the Intellectual Concord and the 8 to the Business-Minded Concord. This Maturity Number can bring new worries about money, and as you age, you may become bossy and hypocritical. This will be a dramatic shift, as it exists in a new concord for you. The change may be straining on your existing relationships.

The Meaning of Your Maturity Number

The Maturity Number is a complex number that I encourage you to think about it in relation to the other numbers in your profile as well as compatibility.

MATURITY NUMBER 1

You will require more independence and individuality and need to fight harder for recognition and rewards. Guard against becoming a bully and combative.

MATURITY NUMBER 2

Your sensitivity will increase as well as your tact and diplomacy. You will work harmoniously behind the scenes and guide gently rather than using force.

MATURITY NUMBER 3

You will become more social and extroverted. Your communication will improve along with your popularity and creative potential. You may take up painting, writing, or acting.

MATURITY NUMBER 4

You will find yourself becoming more of a planner and more practical and organized. Guard against becoming uptight, inflexible, and too opinionated. Remember to make time for fun!

MATURITY NUMBER 5

Travel, freedom, and unexpected events will dominate the second half of your life. Your storytelling abilities will grow, and you will become more original and more of a risk taker. Be careful of scattering your energies.

MATURITY NUMBER 6

Family, friends, and community will be of increasing concern to you. You will mature like a wise sage and be able to provide advice and comfort to those who need it. The 6 Maturity Number promises a secure old age. These are often the children who care for elderly parents.

MATURITY NUMBER 7

You must guard against becoming reclusive. You will spend your time reading and continue to educate yourself while asking life's big questions. Your intuition will grow stronger as will your ability to form unique opinions and conclusions.

MATURITY NUMBER 8

You will learn to detach from material success. Many with this number never really retire, and become consumed by accumulation and greed. You can achieve success and financial independence if you keep your ego in check and focus on humanitarian acts to maintain balance.

MATURITY NUMBER 9

Your wisdom, sense of humor, and humanitarianism will all flourish under this number. Volunteering and an interest in arts and culture will bring you joy. You will strive to provide something of lasting value.

MATURITY NUMBER 11

The 11 will add incredible intuitive and psychic experiences as you age. Learn to trust them. Your sensitivity and judgement of character will deepen. You will be discriminating about whom you allow into your world and will have lasting relationships as a result. (Also read the energy for the 2.)

MATURITY NUMBER 22

This Maturity Number must be reached by having Life Path Number 11 and Destiny Number 11.

With this Maturity Number, you will have a strong foundation, solid intuition, a newfound self-confidence, and deep personal power. These tools will help you bring many dreams into reality and leave a legacy. (Also read the energy for the 4.)

MATURITY NUMBER 33

This Maturity Number must be reached by having 11 and 22 Life Path or Destiny Numbers.

You will bring love into everything you do. You can now bring your vision to life with compassion, focusing your emotional energy on higher goals that align with spiritual teaching. (Also read the energy of the 6.)

Your Maturity Number is something to embrace and look forward to. You are merging your Life Path and Destiny into a powerful sum of experience and ultimate wisdom. You can now direct your life with confidence and finally bring dreams into reality.

Repeating Numbers

Once your Core Profile is complete, you may notice that some numbers repeat—for instance, you may have a Birthday Number 9 and a Soul Number 9, causing you to be condescending at times, or your Destiny and Personality Numbers may both be 1's, making you susceptible to aggression or selfishness. Repeat numbers in your profile will be expressed in an intense way. It's very common to have a double dose of the same number—and I have clients with as many as 5 out of 7 numbers in their profile repeating!

Repeat numbers present both unique challenges and unique opportunities. Once you acknowledge and are aware of a particular intensity in your profile, you can put in the hard work of tempering your reactions and changing your approach to challenges.

Recently, a client told me about their niece who was born on the 9th day and also has a Life Path Number 9. There's nothing wrong with that; however, the name she was given also resulted in 9's for her Destiny, Soul, and Personality Numbers. Given the intense presence of the 9 in her profile, her soul will struggle to find balance and will have to work hard to develop other tools needed to cope and live at the high vibration of the 9. (I couldn't help but think they are raising either a career criminal or Mother Teresa.)

Think of your Core Profile like a toolbox. If you have four to seven unique numbers in your profile, you are working with lots of tools and have a diverse set of skills to draw from. If you have only two to three different numbers, your tools are somewhat limited, and you will have to work extra hard to develop skills outside of your natural abilities.

Now that you have learned who you are, let's explore where you are in the sense of life timing and cycles.

PERSONAL CYCLES: MAKING THE MOST OUT OF EVERY DAY, MONTH, AND YEAR

Now that you have a deep understanding of yourself through the numerical values of your birth date and given name, let's explore what the numbers can reveal about the day, month, and year you are in—and where you are headed.

Numerology works on an evolving pattern of a 9-year cycle and then begins again from 1. Each year of the 9-year cycle carries its own unique demands, rhythm, and patterns. Within each year, there is also a cycle of months and days. The combined energy of your Personal Years, Months, and Days greatly impacts the timing of your life and how things uniquely unfold for you. Understanding these cycles and their respective energies can also help you plan for the future.

Personal Cycles are one of the most exciting aspects of Numerology and are amazingly accurate predictors of the themes, challenges, and opportunities that you'll encounter at a given time. Determining your Attitude Number provides the foundation to unlock the mystery of these cycles.

Your Attitude Number

Before we get into the cycles, we need to identify your Attitude Number, as this plays a role in calculating your personal cycle. This number is about how you present to the world—the attitude and vibration you naturally exude. Many of us like to believe we are devoid of attitude, but everyone has one!

This number comes from the month and day you were born. As you did with your Life Path Number (see page 20), first reduce the month and day to a single digit, then add them together.

MONTH + DAY = ATTITUDE NUMBER

EXAMPLE: *December 1st*

MONTH: *12 (1+2 = 3) so the month number is 3*

BIRTHDAY NUMBER: *1, no reduction necessary so the day number is 1*

3+1=4, so the Attitude Number is 4

September 17th

MONTH: *9, no reduction necessary so the month number is 9*

BIRTHDAY: *17 (1+7=8), so the Birthday Number is 8*

9+8 = 17 (1+7=8), so the Attitude Number is 8

Go ahead and add your Attitude Number to your profile.

The Meaning of Your Attitude Number

Now that you know how to calculate your Attitude Number, let's explore what it means. Understood by others intuitively and without conscious thought, this is where people will decide if they like you or not and if they can vibe with you in a positive way. It's about first impressions and judgments. It makes sense that this number also often gets you hired.

ATTITUDE NUMBER 1

You are an original: You put your unique signature on everything you do. You may come off as aggressive but very confident and capable at the same time. You are full of enthusiasm and great ideas.

You are not afraid of confrontation and can be very impulsive, not always considering the long-term consequences of your actions and decisions.

ATTITUDE NUMBER 2 (OR MASTER NUMBER 11)

Your first impression on others is one of kindness, diplomacy, and patience.

Your incredible sensitivity is often expressed as anxiety. Be aware of what you "pick up" from others. You do not need to take ownership of someone else's experience, mood, opinions, or feelings.

For the Master Number 11, add an intense amount of intuition and even more sensitivity to the 2 character traits. You are a Master Dreamer, an intuitive force. You're at your best when you are inspiring others.

ATTITUDE NUMBER 3

You come across as happy and carefree, but you are very sensitive and secretly fear criticism and disapproval. You can be scattered, often telling more than one story at a time. You love to laugh and make others laugh. You're extremely social, smart, and witty.

You can seem moody and hard on yourself. There's no need to carry that emotional baggage around: Work through it, and don't take everything so personally.

ATTITUDE NUMBER 4 (OR MASTER NUMBER 22)

Emotionally elusive, you must be careful of coming across as unfeeling or cold. Showing vulnerability with your feelings doesn't have to be a weakness. You love rules, justice, and for things to be fair. You appreciate it when others pick up on your organizational and management skills.

Master Number 22 has the energy of the 4, amped up to the powerful Master Builder of the 22. Others will see your great capacity for building something of lasting value. Keep your ego in check: You may appear self-absorbed.

ATTITUDE NUMBER 5

You use your charisma to navigate through and get what you want out of life. You prefer a jet-fueled existence of adventure and fun; you seem to fear nothing and are always looking for a rush. You function best in an environment that's constantly changing, dynamic, and even chaotic. Others will pick up on your intolerance of boredom.

ATTITUDE NUMBER 6 (OR MASTER NUMBER 33)

Capable, smart, and quick-minded, you are great in an emergency and even better at controlling the narrative. A brilliant spin doctor, you know what to do and who to call. Others see you as a perfectionist with great taste who's hesitant to veer from your own perfect vision of things.

ATTITUDE NUMBER 7

You feel like small talk actually could kill you: If it involves fake smiling, you would rather stay home. You love a good spreadsheet. This makes you seem standoffish and aloof. You have an air of mystery about you because you like to keep your cards close. You would much rather observe and ask questions than share anything too personal.

Inquisitive, you prefer one-on-one intellectual conversations over groups talking pleasantries. Your sarcasm and sometimes dry sense of humor is not always well received: Know your audience. People find you intriguing but hard to figure out.

ATTITUDE NUMBER 8

Born to lead, and when balanced, this number is unstoppable. With desires and dedication to spare, your dreams are big, which often sets you up for disappointment. You project confidence and work to maintain a successful image.

At times tactless and opinionated, you despise time wasters. Time is money, after all, and it can provide the stability, security, and freedom you desire. If you find yourself with a lack of resources or control, you can adopt a defeatist attitude and get angry. Karma comes back on you quickly, good or bad.

ATTITUDE NUMBER 9

You have an aura of confidence and charm to spare. People are often intimidated by you. The attitude of the 9 can be polarizing—people will either love you or despise you. Anyone with something to hide will fear that you'll expose them on an unconscious level.

Personal Years and Cycles

It's time for one of the predictive pieces of Numerology. The most relevant and potent cycle that influences your experiences is the Personal Year Cycle. Learning this can make you feel like you have a crystal ball!

Numerology works on an evolving pattern of the 9-year cycle and then begins again with 1. When you are born, you do not necessarily start at the beginning of the 9-year cycle. Your Personal Year is based on the Universal Year in which you which you were born and where that year falls in the cycle. Your Personal Year depends on your Attitude Number and the year you were born.

Each year of the 9-year cycle carries its own unique demands, rhythm, and personality. There are lessons to be learned, options to be weighed, and moments to be seized within each cycle, so knowing where you fall can unlock important mysteries about your life path.

WHAT IS MY CURRENT PERSONAL YEAR?

The first step in calculating your Personal Year is understanding the current Universal Year. This is where our collective energy is found. Everyone feels the energy of the Universal Year to some degree or another. The impact of its vibration is evident in news cycles, major world events, and other highlights that emerge throughout the year.

The Universal Year is simply the calendar year reduced to a single digit. Here are a few examples:

2017   2+0+1+7 = 10 (1+0) = 1

2022   2+0+2+2 = 6

1993   1+9+9+3 = 22/4

When you combine your Attitude Number with the reduced Universal Year, you will find the rhythm for your life. This number reveals the possibilities and prospects of your future.

Attitude Number (Month of Birth + Day of Birth) + Universal Year = Personal Year Number

Let's say your birthday is August 25th.

8 + 25 (2+5) = **7 = 15 (1+5) = 6**

So, your Attitude Number is 6. And we are in the year 2019.

2 +0+1+9 = 12 (1+2) = **3**

6 + 3 = **9 Personal Year**

Your current Personal Year energy will run from January to the end of December. When the Universal calendar advances, so will your personal year. In this case, moving the cycle back to 1.

It is important to be mindful of the "halo effect" that will influence the first three and last three months of any personal year. The new energy of the next year can begin to be felt as soon as October, and the old energy from the previous year lingers around until March. Also note that if you have Attitude Number 9, you will correspond to the energy of the personal year and feel the world's energy more intensely.

The Meaning of Each Personal Year

Every year of the 9-year cycle will be filled with different adventures to help you grow and evolve throughout your life. The unique experiences, challenges, and opportunities of each cycle will all add important knowledge and coping skills to your toolbox.

Some years are easier than others; some feel fast, some slow. Events will make more sense because you can recognize and reflect on them with the perspective of Numerology. Having this information means that your lessons will come easier and your growth will be more seamless.

Take advantage of the predictive powers of the Personal Year and become an active architect of your life.

PERSONAL YEAR 1: THE YEAR OF BEGINNINGS

This is the time to move forward! It is a welcome change after your Year 9, where you were letting go and making room for new beginnings.

With the halo effect you will still feel a few things falling away that you neglected to let go of last year. Year 1 can feel like a slow start. But it is the perfect time to set your intentions, plant seeds, grow your ideas, and begin to initiate action to bring them into reality. What happens now will directly impact your rewards or harvest in your next 9 Year.

There is a newfound confidence available to you now. You have momentum and can really make things happen. This year will create movement and progress and will go by fast. You may find you are more aggressive now. Remember to play well with others, don't be stubborn, and ask for help when you need it.

PERSONAL YEAR 2 AND 11/2: THE YEAR OF RELATIONSHIPS & PATIENCE

This year is the time to nurture the seeds you planted in Year 1. Your time will be best used by tending to those big ideas you set in motion last year.

You will make strong connections and meet people who can help you further your goals and dreams. This is a great time for romantic connections and the expansion of family.

This year moves a little slower than the last, and your patience and ability to compromise will be put to the test. You will experience heightened sensitivity.

Master 11 Year: If you picture the 11 as two 1's coming together (getting married, having a baby) or moving apart (divorce, departure of a loved one), you'll see how this year involves destined relationship events. Your intuition is high, so trust your instincts.

Notice if you are being manipulative, stubborn, or selfish, which stems from the low vibration of the double 1 energy.

PERSONAL YEAR 3: THE YEAR OF SOCIAL & EMOTIONAL EVENTS

Your Personal Year 3 will be a social one, and you may find yourself more popular than usual. 3's are the great connectors: Be open to invitations. The Universe wants to make some connections for you this year! Let them happen. This is your year of "yes." Accept every invitation you get, and meet as many people as you can.

It will also be an emotional year, and this means ALL of the emotions: anger, fear, sadness, joy, frustration, and more. Find a creative outlet you can channel your heightened emotional energy into. Your creativity and communication skills will be at their peak this year.

This is also your date with destiny! In a Year 3 you will likely meet someone who has a major impact on your life or gives you a life-changing opportunity.

The 3 loves expansion. Be cautious not to exaggerate and embellish too much. Be even more cautious about gaining weight.

PERSONAL YEAR 4 & 22/4: THE YEAR OF DISCIPLINE & DETAILS

Many Numerology books will scare you about how much hard work is required in your Personal Year 4. Stay focused and dedicated: it's equally about taking care of details, learning about procrastination, and following the rules. If you break the rules, there will be consequences. If you speed, you get a ticket; if you lie, you're exposed. Be careful not to neglect your health. Stay on top of your annual checkups.

This year is all about letting go and learning to trust the divine. Go with the flow and don't force things, or they will backfire—badly!

Master 22 Year: Year 4 is when you put things in order, creating a foundation to build your dreams upon. Your lessons will include keeping your ego in check and learning to overcome obstacles you cannot control. It will be important for you to trust others as part of your master plans.

PERSONAL YEAR 5: THE YEAR OF CHANGE, FREEDOM & ADVENTURE

In a Year 5 you may begin to feel caged-in and ready for change. This is the midway point in your cycle, and you may be itching for something new. This year it's common to want a new home, car, career, or significant other. The 5 year is a social year and a good time to start a new romantic relationship. It's also a fabulous year to travel, take an adventure, and try new things. Pay special attention to new people and opportunities that come your way.

Be aware of your involvement in drama and gossip this year—you will attract them like a magnet! You also may find you're a little clumsy or accident-prone.

PERSONAL YEAR 6: FAMILY & RESPONSIBILITY

Your Personal Year 6 rules marriage, divorce, birth and death, family, your home, and your pets. The devil/angel quality of the 6 applies to this year as well.

The Year 6 rules education, so you may find yourself going back to school or taking classes or workshops on the weekends. It's a great year to learn something new. Your personal magnetism is strong this year, so it can be a year of romance and successful courtship.

You can expect some of the best and some of the most emotionally difficult events of your life to happen during 6 Years. You might get married and, months later, lose a loved one or pet.

PERSONAL YEAR 7: THE YEAR OF EXPERTISE & SELF-CARE

Now is the time to become the expert on something. Specialize your skills and indulge your curiosity. This is a great year to take a spiritual quest or explore metaphysics.

This is also the year of self-care. Be sure to take time for yourself.

Being in nature or around water will do wonders for your soul. It's also a good time to begin practicing meditation or yoga. You will likely feel reclusive at times this year, preferring to stay home rather than go out. However, you must guard against depression. Year 7 will force you to evaluate your life and feelings.

PERSONAL YEAR 8: THE YEAR OF ACHIEVEMENT, AUTHORITY & MONEY

The Personal Year 8 is all about the revolving door of money. Anything is possible this year—you could win the lottery or declare bankruptcy.

Authority figures, good or bad, are in the front row of your life right now. This is a great year to get promoted or start your own business.

Many rewards are realized in Year 8. These are a direct reflection of the efforts you put in during years 1 through 8. Material gains, success, financial security, and status are all on the table. A word of caution—8 is the number of complete and total reversals, so it's easy to find yourself going from high to low, attainment balanced to your previous efforts.

If you've thought about it, take action now. In Year 9 it will be too late to start new endeavors. This is your last chance to go for it before your 1 Year.

Be cautious of making things more complicated than they need to be. Balance and authenticity are where your magic will be found.

PERSONAL YEAR 9: THE YEAR OF COMPLETION & RELEASE

This is the year to complete things and let go of what no longer serves you. You've reached the end of your 9-year cycle and are primed to receive the rewards from all your growth and hard work.

If you try to start things during a 9 Year, like relationships or a new job, they likely won't stick. Your courage and strength will be tested. Toxic relationships will fall away, and lingering problems can find resolution. This is the time to get closure and heal.

Forgiveness is important now. Release the past to make room for your future. You don't want resentment living rent-free when you have an exciting new tenant in the prospects of your next Year 1. Clear some space to dream big and make plans.

Is There an Attitude Problem?

You know how sometimes you're on the same page with someone and sometimes you're not? This is largely due to your Attitude Number, which determines both your approach to life and your cycles. If you want to examine your compatibility with someone, take a look at your Attitude Numbers together. If your Attitude Numbers are in the same concord (see page 62), you are off to a great start, and most of the time you and this person will be in balance.

The most telling way to reveal disharmony or incompatibility is through Stress Numbers. Calculating a Stress Number is one of the only times you will use subtraction in Numerology. To get there, subtract the smaller Attitude Number from the larger. For example:

You have a 9 Attitude Number and your best friend has a 6 Attitude
         Number.

   9 - 6 = 3

This means you have a 3 Attitude Stress Number between you.

   Stress Numbers reveal your natural stride with another person.
When you are aware of this number, you can use any challenges to your
advantage. It will tell you if you can travel or work together successfully and what it will take to make the relationship work. This applies
to all relationships, partnerships, family, and work connections.

   When it comes to romantic compatibility, you will want to look at the
Soul Stress Number as well, which we explore in chapter 6 (see page 114).

Attitude Stress Number 1: You will need to have independence
         between you and appreciate the individual. Guard against
         being selfish or stubborn.

Attitude Stress Number 2: You will need to practice patience
         with one another, be sensitive to each other's needs, and
         compromise.

Attitude Stress Number 3: You will need to share fun experiences,
         be sensitive to emotions, and not say things you cannot
         come back from. Good communication is key here to avoid
         misunderstandings.

Attitude Stress Number 4: This can take some work. You will have to
         guard against being controlling and inflexible. Vulnerabil-
         ity with feelings, good boundaries, and a willingness to put
         in the work will be necessary.

Attitude Stress Number 5: You may have a nontraditional relation-
         ship, as one or both of you may have a need for freedom.
         You will also have to keep things interesting and enter-
         taining. Monotony and routine will be problematic for this

relationship. Boredom can lead to some epic battles. Avoid unnecessary drama.

Attitude Stress Number 6: Family issues can overtake this relationship, leaving the other person feeling like a second choice. Avoid inflexible opinions. You will both have to be responsible and stop keeping score.

Attitude Stress Number 7: Within this pairing, each person requires alone time. You can spend significant time together not speaking, just enjoying each other's energy while each doing your own thing. A spiritual foundation of some kind is important here.

Attitude Stress Number 8: There can be power struggles here. For this relationship to work best, you both need to let the other rule at the appropriate time, supporting instead of fighting. Your relationship may feel like it's all business. Money can be an issue.

Attitude Stress Number 0: This relationship is a mirror. It tends to work because you want the same things at the same time. On the other hand, your bad habits will also be reflected back. This relationship can become a narcissistic one, where the other person is only admired for the qualities they share. Identify your bad habits, and you will find real personal growth within this relationship.

Age Vibration

I believe the current age of a person should be looked at as its own unique vibration.

To find your Age Vibration, add and reduce the digits in your age together to reach a single digit. For example, if you are 43 (4+3) = 7, you are experiencing a 7 Age Vibration.

Apply what you have learned about the energy of the Personal Year cycles to this number. This energy will be an undercurrent to your Personal Year. Your Age Vibration will run from one birthday to the next, when you will recalculate it.

Pay special attention to your Master Number Age Vibrations, such as, 22, 33, 44, 55, 66, and so on. These years hold destined and significant events!

Personal Months and Cycles

While your Personal Year reveals the theme of the life cycle you're in, the Personal Month is a secondary energy to help you complete your tasks and lessons. Personal Months are like added spice on your Personal Year energy. In turn, each Personal Year gives a different flavor to your Personal Months. These two numbers work in harmony, guiding you along your soul's growth journey.

WHAT IS MY CURRENT PERSONAL MONTH?

Your Personal Month also works on the 1 to 9 cycle. To calculate your Personal Month:

Current Personal Year + Current Calendar Month

For example, you are in a 5 Personal Year and it is currently the month of July. July is the 7th month, so:

Personal Year 5 + Month 7 = 12 (1+2) = 3

You are in a Personal Month 3.

Or say you are in a Personal Year 7 and it is currently April, the 4th month of the year:

7 + 4 = 11/2

You are in an Personal Month 11/2.

The Meaning of Your Personal Month

Once you are familiar with the unique tools that each month brings, you can plan accordingly. Use the energy that is available to you! For instance, in your Month 1 get your game plan together, promote yourself in your Month 3, sell your idea in your Month 5, and plan to visit family in your Month 6.

Since everything in Numerology works on the cycle of 9 and there are 12 months in the year, there are 3 months in every year when you will experience repeat Numerological energy. January, February, and March hold the same energy as October, November and December.

The halo effect provides a fresh vibration for the second round of these numbers.

PERSONAL MONTH 1

Just begin! Start something new and manifest your plans with the New Moon.

PERSONAL MONTH 2 (OR MASTER 11)

This month's focus will be on relationships. Cooperate and be patient.

PERSONAL MONTH 3

This month is your date with destiny. Socialize, have fun, and find a creative outlet. Your emotions will be running high.

PERSONAL MONTH 4

Don't procrastinate! Take care of details and anything you've left undone. Stay on top of your health.

PERSONAL MONTH 5

Avoid gossip and drama. Embrace change. You may be clumsy and accident-prone this month.

PERSONAL MONTH 6

Beautify your surroundings. Focus on family and pets.

PERSONAL MONTH 7

Become the expert on something. Investigate and research. Self-care is important now. You may feel reclusive.

PERSONAL MONTH 8

This month brings the revolving door of money: There may be a bonus or unexpected funds coming your way. Watch out—it will leave just as quickly due to unforeseen expenses.

PERSONAL MONTH 9

Forgive, get rid of things, donate your time and money, and perform random acts of kindness. Collect your reward! Work with the Full Moon to release and make room for new blessings in your next 9-month cycle.

The Magic of October

September is the 9th month, meaning it will always be the same as your Personal Year. During this month your Personal Year and Month are intensified. By October, you'll be ready for some relief.

Pay special attention to the month of October. It is the best fortune-teller of things to come. It holds the numerical vibration of what will be your theme for your next Personal Year. You can mindfully influence this energy by sending messages to the Universe of what you desire and want to call in.

If you have trouble getting places on time, be punctual in October, and it will be less of a struggle in the following year. Want more time to read? Make time for reading now and the habit will stick. If you set the tone in October, the Universe will help you achieve what you've set out to do for the rest of your year. Pay attention to unexpected and unplanned events—think injuries, chance meetings, or travel delays— these are hints of what will come next year.

I'm equally diligent about what I don't want more of: I don't take my dog to the vet, go to the dentist, or take my car for so much as an oil change. I don't want more of any of those things in my year unless absolutely necessary.

Fill October with what you love, and set clear intentions. This goes for every October, for everyone!

Most & Least Compatible Cycles

Certain months and days will flow better within certain years than others. Some work very harmoniously together; some are in opposition.

For example, If you are in a 7 Year and 3 Month, these two numbers want different things. The Personal Year 7 may be making you feel reclusive while the 3 wants to be very social, causing inner turmoil. The 7 also rules your mental faculties and depression; when combined with the emotional energy of the 3, you may hit a whole new level of feelings you didn't even know you had.

The Personal Month 1's (there will be two) of your Personal Year 9 can create a real push/pull in your life. The 9 wants to bring things to completion while the aggressive 1 energy wants to begin new things.

Learning how to balance these two powerful energies and taking advantage of their vibrations are the best ways for you to find fulfillment throughout the year and achieve your goals.

When you are in a numerically compatible cycle, it is a great opportunity for progress and success. For example, a 4 Month of an 8 Year can bring organization to your taxes or paperwork. The 4 provides the natural energy for details and discipline, and the 8 will help you tap into the tools to complete projects or create a strong foundation for business and career.

The 9 Month of a 6 Year can give you the motivation to complete a home project or renovation. You'll finally be able to realize and enjoy your creative vision.

Compatible cycles don't mean that problems go away, but when your cycles are in harmony, even difficult situations will feel easier to navigate and offer more opportunities to change and grow.

Personal Days and Cycles

Personal Days are the final layer of your cycle. You feel the energy of the days less than your Personal Year or Personal Month, but they do hold important information that can guide you in choosing special dates, such as when to have important conversations or surgeries, plan an event like a wedding, or take certain action.

The best way to understand the impact of personal days is to pay attention to personal events. For example, you may get a raise on an 8 Day or go on a fabulous date on an 11/2 Day or a 6. You will learn which days work best for you and what each day is best for.

WHAT IS MY CURRENT PERSONAL DAY?

To calculate your Personal Day, add the calendar day to your Personal Month (see page 83).

Personal Month + Calendar Day

For example, let's say it is March 6th and you are in a Personal Year 5. March is the 3rd month of the year, so:

Personal Year 5 + 3rd Month = Personal Month 8

Personal Month 8 + Calendar Day 6 = Personal Day 14/5

Or, it is December 15 and you are in a Personal Year 4. December is the 12th month, so:

Personal Year 4 + 12th Month (1+2=3) = Personal Month 7

Personal Month 7 + 15 (1+5) = Calendar Day 6 = Personal Day 13/4

The Meaning of Your Personal Days

Being aware of your Personal Day illuminates the subtleties of life. Your Personal Year and Month add a special spin to each day.

PERSONAL DAY 1

This is a day of great ideas, a day to begin something. Focus on self, but don't be selfish or stubborn. It's time to be decisive and ambitious and take confident action.

PERSONAL DAY 2

Be patient and tend to details. Work on relationships and cooperation. This is a gentle day. You'll feel sensitive and intuitive and may have vivid dreams.

PERSONAL DAY 3

Be creative, spend time with friends, and communicate. Accept any invitations you receive. Practice gratitude. Avoid entitled behavior. This is a lucky day!

PERSONAL DAY 4

Get organized. Focus on your health. Guard against being rigid, uptight, or controlling. Don't procrastinate. Take care of details to move closer to your goal. Follow the rules or face the consequences.

PERSONAL DAY 5

Make a change, network, or promote. Guard against being too impulsive. Focus your energy. Be ready for change; the day may not go as planned.

PERSONAL DAY 6

Pay attention to your family, pets, and home. Beautify something. Be mindful of your own strong opinions. Focus on domestic matters and channel your nurturing energy. See your therapist, get your hair done, learn something new.

PERSONAL DAY 7

This is time for quiet solitude. Rest and reevaluate. Meditate. Spend time outdoors, near water, or reading. You may feel reclusive. Self-care is a priority.

PERSONAL DAY 8

Handle money, ask for a raise, collect your debts, pay bills, take charge. Be careful not to repeat lessons or mistakes. Take care of business for progress and success. Karma finds balance today. You may have issues with authority figures.

PERSONAL DAY 9

Wrap things up. Release and forgive. Practice random acts of kindness. Give something away. Finalize projects and details.

Bringing It All Together

Whether you are aware of the cycle or not, your life is unfolding in a distinct pattern of events helping you move along your personal growth highway.

Now that you know about the themes and patterns of your 9-year cycles, you can spot windows of opportunity and avoid unnecessary turmoil.

Mapping out your year doesn't have to be complex. Set reminders, write on a calendar, and make notes in your phone, and eventually it will become second nature. Consulting the numbers of your Personal Year, Month, and Day before making big decisions or changes will give you clarity, focus, and peace of mind.

It really is all in the numbers! And there's even more to be revealed . . .

5

REVEALING CHARTS & ARROWS

Now we'll move into the intriguing practice of charting significant numbers and exploring what these charts reveal about a person's inner nature. Specifically, I'll teach you how to create a Birth Chart and a Name Chart and how to interpret the "arrows" on these charts to deepen your numerical knowledge. These grids originate from the magical discipline of Arithmancy. The word *arithmancy* comes from the Greek word *arithmos*, meaning number, and *mantia*, meaning divination. Arithmancy is the study of divination through numbers.

You may recall Hermione Granger taking Arithmancy classes in the Harry Potter books. In our world, Numerology and Arithmancy are closely related. It's not just for wizards! All you need is your paper and pencil.

Creating Your Birth Chart

When combined with other Arithmancy calculations, the Birth Chart reveals important character strengths and shadows. Birth Charts are also often referred to as Karmic Numerology, Arrows of Pythagoras, Energy Lines, the Lo Shu or Magical Square (Chinese Arithmancy), and Lines of Pythagoras. Grid arithmancy was developed independently of Pythagorean teachings, but also uses the 1 through 9 system. Personally, I find the interpretations in these charts very broad, but they can bring a new layer of understanding to your readings.

To create your Birth Chart, first draw a 3 x 3-square grid that can hold the numbers 1 through 9 like the example below. Then fill in the numbers of your birth date ONLY. Unlike the other calculations we have done, DO NOT reduce. Use two digits for the month, two digits for the day, and four digits for the year. Place any 1's in the bottom left square, 5's in the center square, and so on, until you have the full date mapped on your chart. Any zeroes go outside of the chart along the bottom edge.

3	6	9
2	5	8
1	4	7

0

Here you are practicing an Arithmancy grid.

Let's look at a few example charts:

Elvis Presley

Birthdate: January 8, 1935 (01 08 1935)

3		9
	5	8
11		

00

Stevie Nicks

Birthdate: May 26, 1948 (05 26 1948)

	6	9
2	5	8
1	4	
	0	

Lady Gaga

Birthdate: March 28, 1986 (03 28 1986)

3	6	9
2		88
1		
	0	

The blank squares in your Birth Chart represent Karmic Lessons (see page 60). Check which squares are empty for you and refer back to the significance of each number when it comes to these lessons. You will encounter similar struggles and challenges again and again until you master these lessons.

The 0's at the bottom of the Birth Chart represent unresolved Karmic Debts that a person has accumulated from previous incarnations. The more 0's, the more Karmic Debt a person has. These debts must be paid in this lifetime if you do not want to carry them into the next.

The Meaning of Your Birth Chart

The meanings of the numbers in Birth Charts are similar to the classic meanings of Numerology with some added nuances. The meaning of the overall chart is revealed through the placement of the numbers— where they fall in rows, columns, and on the diagonal. Full horizontal lines show strength in the Mental, Emotional, and Physical realms. Missing numbers reveal a weakness in a particular plane.

Birth Chart numbers represent:

1 - Ego, identity, resourcefulness, leadership

2 - Duality, sensitivity, imbalance, the conscious mind

3 - Creativity, assertiveness, initiative, action, service

4 - Practicality, instincts, logic, materialism

5 - Flexibility, tolerance, adaptability, willingness to learn, the five senses

6 - Imagination, fantasy, original ideas

7 - Boundaries, time, material attachments, spirituality

8 - The unconscious mind, balance, material transformation

9 - Selflessness, romance, wisdom, generosity, artistic talents

TOP ROW: THE MENTAL PLANE 3, 6 & 9

This row rules intellect, thought, ideas, creativity, innovation, imagination, and analyzing. Having all numbers in this row means you have good judgment. If you are missing numbers in this row, you will demonstrate poor reasoning and may not be very dynamic.

MIDDLE ROW: THE SOUL OR EMOTIONAL PLANE 2, 5 & 8

This plane rules sensitivity, emotions, and spirituality. When you have all the numbers in this row, you are emotionally balanced, artistic, and intuitive. If you have missing numbers in this row, you will show degrees of emotional confusion and be overly sensitive.

BOTTOM ROW: THE PHYSICAL PLANE 1, 4 & 7

Having all the numbers present in the bottom row suggests good health, strength, and physical skillfulness. If all or some of the numbers are absent, it reveals an impractical and awkward character.

Arrows in Birth Charts

There are eight possible lines of numbers that can be formed in the grid: three horizontal, three vertical, and two diagonal lines. These are called the Arrows of Strength. Having any set of complete lines is a little like possessing a superpower. These arrows represent inherent or genetic strength and extra skills or gifts in a specific area. You can tap into these gifts when faced with a stressful or difficult situation and they will help make your life flow.

There are also eight possible *empty* lines that can be formed from missing numbers: three horizontal, three vertical, and two diagonal lines. These are called the Arrows of Weakness. These arrows create challenges in a specific area. If you're missing a complete number line, you may have to work harder to balance some aspects of your character. The lessons from these empty arrows illuminate opportunity for growth and soul evolution.

You may not have any complete or completely missing lines. That's okay. Without any empty lines, your lessons will be less obvious and less intense.

Reviewing all your arrows together tells the whole story. Let's take a look.

There are a total of 16 possible arrows, and every chart will have at least two empty squares.

ARROW OF DETERMINATION: 1, 5, 9

Determination, persistence, willpower, drive, or ability to overcome adversity.

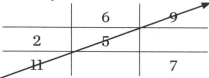

ARROW OF RESIGNATION: MISSING 1, 5, 9

Lack of motivation, indecisiveness, shyness, indifference, and surrender.

(No one born in the years 1889 to 1999 will have this Arrow of Weakness.)

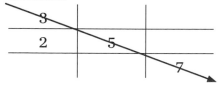

ARROW OF SPIRITUALITY: 3, 5, 7

Compassion, spirituality, faith, strong convictions, and hidden intuition.

ARROW OF SKEPTICISM, MISSING: 3, 5, 7

Lack of spirituality, little emotional awareness, doubt.

ARROW OF INTELLECT: 3, 6, 9

Intelligence, logic, exceptional memory, researcher, problem solver.

3	6	9	→
1		7	

ARROW OF POOR MEMORY: MISSING 3, 6, 9

Forgetfulness, poor concentration, lack of sympathy, disinterest, avoidance of responsibility.

(No one born between 1889 to 1999 has this Arrow of Weakness.)

22		8	→
1	4		

ARROW OF EMOTIONAL BALANCE: 2, 5, 8

Exaggerated emotion, empathy, neediness, seriousness.

	6		
2	5	8	→
1			

ARROW OF HYPERSENSITIVITY: MISSING 2, 5, 8

Sensitivity, feelings of inferiority, intimidation, a longing to heal.

(This Arrow of Weakness will not appear again until the year 3000.)

	66	9	→
11		7	

ARROW OF PRACTICALITY: 1, 4, 7

Music, creativity, work done with hands, financial responsibility.

	6	9
2		
1	4	7 →

ARROW OF IMPRACTICALITY: MISSING 1, 4, 7

Dreams, impracticality, excessive spending, health problems.

(No one born between 1000 and 1999 has this Arrow of Weakness. For those born after 2000, we will see this impractical arrow.)

	6	99
2		
		→

ARROW OF THE PLANNER: 1, 2, 3

Organization, discipline, skill, achievement.

3		99
2	5	
1		

ARROW OF CONFUSION: MISSING 1, 2, 3

Confusion, lack of organization, lack of commitment, misunderstandings.

(This Arrow of Weakness will not appear again until the year 4000.)

	6	99
	4	

ARROW OF THE WILL: 4, 5, 6

Determination, willpower, focus, perseverance, steadfastness.

	6	9
	5	
1	4	

ARROW OF FRUSTRATION: MISSING 4, 5, 6

Disappointment, indecisiveness, resistance to change, hard work, challenges, setbacks.

3		99
2		8
1		

ARROW OF ACTIVITY: 7, 8, 9

Stamina (mental and physical), energy, activity.

	6	9
		8
11		7

ARROW OF HESITATION: MISSING 7, 8, 9

Procrastination, laziness, lack of faith, disorganization.

(No one born between 1667 and 1999 has this Arrow of Weakness.)

3		
2	55	
1		

You can derive many possible meanings and combinations from Birth Charts. Use them in your Numerology practice and you will gain greater understanding of yourself and others!

Creating Your Name Chart

The Name Chart is even richer in information than the Birth Chart. To create your Name Chart, write your full given name on a sheet of paper and, underneath each letter, write the correlating number value (see Letters & Their Numbers, page 41).

Now chart these numbers into a blank 3 x 3 grid, the same way you did for your Birth Chart. Note that Master Numbers are excluded from Name Charts.

Here's an example:

```
E  L  V  I  S      A  A  R  O  N      P  R  E  S  L  E  Y
5  3  4  9  1      1  1  9  6  5      7  9  5  1  3  5  7
```

Now chart the numbers into a blank 3 x 3 grid, the same way you did for your birth date.

Elvis's name chart looks like this:

33	6	999
	5555	
1111	4	77

The Meaning of Your Name Chart

The first thing you will notice in your Name Chart are the missing or empty squares. These reveal the Karmic Lessons (see page 60) that arise from the numbers not represented in your full name. Elvis's chart reveals the lesson of the 2 and the lesson of the 8.

The second thing you can learn from a Name Chart is a person's Intensity Number. This is the most repeated number found in your Name Chart and reveals character traits that are more intense than others. For instance, in Elvis's chart you see four 1's and four 5's.

Let's examine each number in the Name Chart.

INTENSITY 1

On average, people have one to three 1's in their name. If this is the case, you will be assertive and driven. With more than four 1's, you will be considered strong and independent and will stand out in a crowd. Six or more is considered an over-intensification, causing you to be aggressive, competitive, stubborn, overbearing, and possibly prone to headaches.

If you are missing 1's, you will lack confidence and independence.

INTENSITY 2

The average number of 2's in a chart is one. This will make you considerate, willing to help, and sensitive to others. If you have more than two 2's you will also be tactful and detailed, have a good sense of rhythm and timing, and have the ability to bring people together. The more 2's you have, the more sensitive you will be.

If you are missing 2's, you will be both impatient and inconsiderate.

INTENSITY 3

Having one or two 3's in your chart will allow you to express yourself and your feelings and give you the ability to have fun. More than three 3's means you will be boastful, artistic, gifted with words, and a little scattered. You may have trouble maintaining focus.

If you are missing 3's, you will struggle with communication and expressing yourself.

INTENSITY 4

Having the average number of two 4's in your name will give you practicality and the ability to see things through. Having three to five 4's will give you unique skills to build things with lasting impact and value. Having more than five 4's is an intensification and will make you controlling, uptight, stubborn, and a workaholic.

If you are missing 4's, you will struggle to stay organized and follow through. Concentration will be difficult for you.

INTENSITY 5

A common number, the average number of 5's in a name is five, which will result in resourcefulness and adaptability. Having more 5's will intensify the power of this number, making you dramatic and prone to addiction, and you have difficulty completing tasks.

If you are missing 5's or have only one, you will not be adaptable and will dislike change and crowds, which may cause you to become reclusive.

INTENSITY 6

If you have one or two 6's, you'll have no trouble taking responsibility in domestic and family matters and finding balance in life. Having three or four 6's indicates strong opinions and a dominant character and means you can be demanding. Having five or more 6's is considered intense. You may struggle with taking on too much responsibility. You may find yourself being taken for granted or taken advantage of.

If you are missing 6's you will lack responsibility, be idealistic, and have unrealistic expectations.

INTENSITY 7

Having one 7 in your name is average and will give you a curious and intuitive nature. Two or more 7's intensifies the number and means you will dislike showing emotion, have a technical mind, and be mysterious and private.

Missing 7's in a Name Chart is very common. It will cause you to be open-minded and not suspicious or paranoid. It may also mean you are impulsive and lack spirituality in your life.

INTENSITY 8

One is the average number of 8's in a name and means you will be competent and able to take charge when necessary. Two or more 8's can give you a good understanding of money but also give money too much power in your life.

If you are missing 8's, you may be reckless with your resources, and your lessons will be found in the realms of money and power.

INTENSITY 9

Having two or three 9's is considered intense and will bring you understanding, creative gifts, and a humanitarian approach to life. If you have only one 9, you may lack awareness of other people's feelings.

Missing 9's will make you self-involved. You will be tested with lessons of tolerance and selfless giving.

Arrows in Your Name Chart

To identify the arrows in your Name Chart, chart your first, middle, and family name separately. Place each on its own grid. The meanings of the arrows remain the same (see page 97). Whichever name you use the most, like your first name, the more the arrows in that name will become dominant in your character. You can also chart nicknames and business names using the same method.

Here's an example:

E	L	V	I	S
5	3	4	9	1

3		9
	5	
1	4	

A	A	R	O	N
1	1	9	6	5

	6	9
	5	
11		

P	R	E	S	L	E	Y
7	9	5	1	3	5	7

3		9
	55	
1		7

As you can see, patterns begin to emerge. Elvis has the arrow of 1, 5, 9 in all three of his names, representing 3 strong Arrows of Determination.

All Your Charts

These charts reveal illuminating information that will complement the five Core Numbers in your profile.

Grids and charts are fascinating because they can help reveal patterns in your life. For instance, you may notice that you are attracted to men who have the same arrows as your father or that everyone in your circle of friends shares similar arrows.

These charts are especially useful when you have limited information about someone, like a coworker. You can chart a first and last name even without the birth date and original birth certificate name.

There are many more complex numerological formulas that can further expand your knowledge of strengths and challenges if you decide to continue your journey into Numerology (see Resources, page 147).

In the next chapter we'll look at bringing all your new fabulous knowledge together and applying it to compatibility, pets, and more!

BRINGING IT ALL TOGETHER: DECODING YOUR FUTURE, COMPATIBILITY, AND RELATIONSHIPS

I t's time to blend all of your new numerical knowledge to decode your future and your relationships. The more readings you do and the more unique charts you explore, the more accurate and confident your readings will be. Numerology, when interpreted responsibly, will give you meaningful insight into others and into the future.

Although one number on its own can give you some information into a person's character, it's limited and may lead you to make false assumptions. You must go deeper if you can, always examining the five Core Numbers together. The five Core Numbers are your:

Life Path Number (page 20)

Soul Number (page 51)

Personality Number (page 53)

Destiny Number (page 40)

Birthday Number (page 12)

These are the foundation for any reading. All of these numbers should already be written in your Core Profile from the work we've done in the previous chapters. The Predictive Cycles, Attitude Number, and Maturity Number provide significant complementary information and round out any profile.

Where to Look

When looking at the Core Numbers together, the first thing you want to do is identify any patterns and contradictions. Here's a quick checklist to help:

- Watch for repeating numbers. Any time a number appears more than once in a Core Profile, you are dealing with a double dose of intense energy, and it may overshadow the whole reading. Always take time to look at the whole chart before you come to conclusions.

- Identify conflicting numbers, which can cause an identity crisis. When key Core Numbers are in contradiction with one another, they will not present as strongly as you may assume. If someone has a Life Path 2, a Personality 1, and a Destiny 1 with a Soul Number 9, there is a lot going on. It's up to you to tactfully interpret these contradictions and draw out the true nature of the person you're reading.

- Pay attention to the vibes. If someone you're reading is living in their shadow self, they may lack the self-awareness to acknowledge who they really are, and a reading may not resonate with them. They are living in ego and are attached to the image they want to project (and protect).

Always view the reading experience of another's soul as a privilege. It is an exercise in intuition and a learning opportunity that will almost always contain a message for you also.

Start with You

Understanding yourself is what will really determine how successful you will be at reading Numerology charts for others. Self-awareness is a skill to be developed just like any other.

If you can't look at all sides of yourself, including your shadow side, you will miss your lessons and avenues for healing. If you find yourself cherry-picking the good in your own chart, your first step is to work on yourself before doing readings for anybody else.

Only when you truly understand yourself will you truly understand the mysteries that Numerology can unlock. You must face the mirror yourself before you hold it up to others. This will bring more sensitivity, empathy, compassion, and intuitive powers to your readings. And when you begin sharing the more shadowy parts of a reading with someone else, do so delicately. Always be willing to offer a solution or path for personal learning.

HOME AND FAMILY

One of the areas where Numerology can be the most helpful is within family relationships, which tend to be intense and complex. Families usually hold deeply rooted patterns. Plus, these are our closest relationships, and the closest relationships are often the most reflective. Patterns in family reveal patterns and habits in the self. Often, it is easier to focus on the bad rather than the good. Remember, you have chosen to incarnate together as a family.

For example, if your mother is a Life Path 6, and you have a Birthday 6, strong opinions will be part of almost every conversation you two have. You may notice that she speaks in absolutes, stating opinions as fact. Do you also do this? Once you recognize it, you can adjust your language and learn to adapt your arguments to be less aggressive.

Families can have some epic battles and long-forgotten skeletons. Approaching these relationships with compassion and understanding will be the key to healing family scars, even those that have existed for generations. Once you have the big picture, you'll be able to navigate these relationships, patterns, and habits more successfully.

WORK AND CAREER

Your career is another area where Numerology is extremely valuable. If I had been aware of these revealing powers early on in my corporate career, I could have saved myself a lot of grief.

For yourself, you can discover your own inherent abilities and create a career path that will bring satisfaction and success. You'll come to understand the types of people you work well with, whom you can trust, and how to overcome difficult relationships and personalities in business.

If you can then access the information required for Numerology from coworkers, you can use it to form unstoppable teams, place people in positions that utilize their natural talents, and understand cycles for initiating projects.

The Life Path and Birthday Numbers will give you an overall sense of people and natural abilities. The Destiny and Personality numbers speak specifically to careers. You will want to pay special attention to these numbers in the workplace.

SPIRITUALITY

Part of the human experience is navigating and developing your own spirituality, which can be a deeply personal and rewarding journey.

Many people are introduced to a specific religion at a young age. As you grow, it is important to explore other paths to discover what really resonates with your own soul.

At first you may be uncertain if there is room for metaphysical practices like Numerology, Astrology, and Tarot within your religious beliefs; some people may assume these practices are evil. But religion and metaphysics can coexist and often deepen rather than dampen the spiritual experience on earth. In fact, there are many Numerological references in spiritual texts like the Bible.

Your Soul Number (page 51), or secret self, is where you will find the keys to decoding your own spiritual beliefs and practices. Your Personal Year 7 or Personal Month 7 is a wonderful time to get in touch with and explore this part of yourself. As you do this, always respect the personal journey and religious practices of others.

Friends

Friendships often end up being some of our most significant and complicated relationships and can be our biggest teachers. Friendships teach us about trust, sharing experiences, empathy, compromise, giving, and receiving. They can be a source of enormous love and respect—a relationship you're in purely by choice. Sadly, they can also teach us about betrayal, entitlement, flakiness, pettiness, gossip, and money issues.

There are different types of friendships. For emotional, heartfelt connections—those people you may consider your "best friends"—you will want to look at the Stress Number that exists between your Soul Numbers, much like a romantic relationship. (We'll get to this soon; see page 114.)

For the relationships that exist between you and your work friends, there will be a different tone. Looking at the Stress Numbers that exist between your Life Path, Birthday and Destiny Numbers will be most revealing.

Stress Numbers help reveal what's required for the friendship to work and the tools you will need to overcome your differences.

In my own life, I've found that friendships with people with similar numerical profiles have ended in very similar ways. I'm sure you've heard it before: "People come into your life for a reason, a season, or a lifetime." You will continue to attract the same personalities until you've learned the lesson you need to learn.

Romance and Significant Others

There are many ways you can numerically connect to your mate. Some matches are more desirable and harmonious than others.

If you are looking for a heartfelt, emotional, soulful romantic connection, you want to make sure that your Life Path and Soul Numbers are harmonious with the other person.

Look for a minimum of three of the five Core Numbers to be from the same concord (see page 62). Ideally, you will have at least one matching number as well, though not necessarily in the same category.

If your Life Path and Soul Number match or your Birthday Number or Soul Number match, it is a magical occurrence! This means you are similar and compatible but will challenge each other in important ways. For example, let's say one person has a Life Path Number 9 with a Soul Number 6 and their partner is a Life Path Number 6 with a Soul Number 9. The Life Path 9 will ground the idealistic 6. The Soul Number 6 will give the Life Path 9 a safe place to be emotionally vulnerable and heal old scars. They will find each other hilarious and appreciate the other's sense of humor. If you have similar profiles, with numbers matching straight across, you will find it easy to love qualities in your partner that you see in yourself. However, these relationships often become toxic and competitive, with one person believing they are superior.

SOUL STRESS NUMBERS

The other important indicator for harmony and success in a relationship is the stress points between Soul Numbers. To find your Soul Stress Number with another person, subtract the smaller Soul Number from the larger. If you have a Soul Number 9 and you are dating someone with a Soul Number of 6, your Stress Number is 3. These numbers say a lot about your potential compatibility and can reveal the best way to resolve conflicts. Note that the Soul Stress Number has an impact on all close relationships (such as a parent and child), not just romantic ones.

SOUL STRESS NUMBER 1: This relationship requires independence in order to work. You will need your own friends and hobbies outside of the relationship. Respect the need to spend time apart and you will be better together! Be aware of selfish tendencies and power struggles. You must both feel that you are equally empowered or in charge. Balance the power and aim to be supportive, not competitive, with each other.

SOUL STRESS NUMBER 2: You make a great team, although you must make sure that you do not compromise too much, becoming resentful. You are both incredibly sensitive and aware of your partner's needs and desires. This energy doesn't like to fight, so minimize conflict as much as possible. Even though there won't be a lot of arguing, this relationship can be enabling and emotionally indulgent.

SOUL STRESS NUMBER 3: Open, honest communication is what will make this relationship work. Secrets or omissions will be extremely damaging. Strive to be sensitive to the other's emotions. Don't use things that have been done or said in the past against the other. Be sure to recognize all your partner does for you and show appreciation. This couple is great at a party. They love to laugh and have fun.

SOUL STRESS NUMBER 4: This relationship can have a lot of rules. You will need good boundaries with each other, and both will want to work on being more flexible. This relationship can feel like it's all business and require mindful effort. Try to have some spontaneous fun together once in a while. Working toward a shared goal can be immensely satisfying for this pair.

SOUL STRESS NUMBER 5: This is a unique relationship, and you may have very different interests, hobbies, or adventures. Frequent and constant change will be a common theme here. Check in often to make sure you are on the same page about expectations and freedom. Avoid "fake drama" instigated to entertain your shared need for excitement. The integrity of this relationship depends on respecting boundaries and establishing mutual trust. Remember your safe word.

SOUL STRESS NUMBER 6: Perfectionism and having idealistic or unrealistic expectations of your partner can cause major problems in this relationship. You will both struggle with taking responsibility and must avoid being self-righteous. You may find that family meddles in your relationship. Be sure to take a step back and talk about issues, as unresolved emotions can be very damaging.

SOUL STRESS NUMBER 7: A spiritual foundation is essential to making this relationship work. You will need to always strive for deep, respectful, meaningful conversation. No gossip and fluff here. Prioritize alone time, and try to avoid overanalyzing every little thing in the relationship. Guard against jealousy.

SOUL STRESS NUMBER 8: You must always maintain utmost respect for each other, otherwise this can become a very competitive "tit for tat" relationship. You will have power struggles that can turn destructive if not managed. If you empower and support one another, you can avoid many of these petty struggles, otherwise the same issues over money, authority, and control will play out on repeat. Money and material attainment will be a focus for this couple.

SOUL STRESS NUMBER 0: When your numbers match, you are in an "all or nothing" relationship. The zero, or cipher, amplifies everything, so there will be a lot of drama, or no drama at all. There is great potential for a dynamic, personal, and spiritual relationship full of growth. The trick is remaining mindful and aware of the other's needs.

After the Stress Numbers, take a look at both of your Maturity Numbers (see page 63). These provide a glimpse at what your partnership will look like later in life. Divorces after the mid-40's can usually be attributed to a major change in one or both Maturity Numbers. Pay careful attention to this number if you are looking at the potential for later-in-life marriages or partnerships.

Meeting People for the First Time

Now that you've opened the Pandora's box of Numerology, there is no going back. You will be applying Numerology to all of your interactions!

When meeting new people, first pay attention to the Attitude Number (first impressions) and the Personality Number (the external self). These can give you a superficial sense of someone's character, mostly revealing their image, not their true motivations or character. Eventually, you will find that you can guess people's numbers based on appearances. 3's have beautiful smiles and often have visible tattoos; 4's often wear glasses and have short, practical haircuts; 8's often wear designer items.

Next, examine their Life Path and Birthday Numbers. These are difficult for people to hide once you start to interact in a meaningful way. Looking at all five numbers in their Core Profile is the only way to get the full picture, and this may take some time.

Be careful of drawing conclusions before looking at a complete chart. Always keep in mind the impact of repeating numbers and numbers in conflict. In addition to their Core Numbers, listen carefully to your intuition.

Pets

Numerology is not just for people! You can apply it to your pets the same way you apply it to yourself. It reveals their unique personalities and what you will experience or learn from them.

Even if you rescue your furry family members from a shelter and don't know their original birth date or given name, that's okay! The name you give them will carry the most significant vibrations. If you do have a date of birth, you can build a full Numerology Profile. But if not, learn what you can from their name—you'll be surprised how much better you understand your pet after this.

Here is a quick reference to pet numbers:

PET NUMBER 1: This is an independent animal, likely an "only child" (or would prefer to be one). This pet is protective and does best when given some type of job, like guard duty.

PET NUMBER 2: This animal is a lover, prefers companionship, and does not like to be left alone. They will be sensitive to discipline and intuitive to their environment. As a result, they may also experience intense anxiety.

PET NUMBER 3: This pet is highly social and likes mischief. They require a lot of attention and have an innate sense of humor. Pet Number 3's will keep you entertained and remind you not to take everything so seriously.

PET NUMBER 4: This is a loyal and obedient companion that plays by the rules. It is all about routine.

PET NUMBER 5: Get a fence! This is an adventurous spirit who wants to explore. This pet bores easily, which can cause it to be destructive and accident-prone. It needs lots of extra stimulation and may like food and treats a little too much.

PET NUMBER 6: This pet is sweet, nurturing, and caring toward any family member who might need a little TLC. Pet Number 6's may actually enjoy "dressing up" and will go anywhere with you, always happy to be included.

PET NUMBER 7: This is a soulful pet. You may actually believe your pet "sees dead people," barking or meowing at apparently nothing. This pet is a bit of a loner and may experience depression.

PET NUMBER 8: This animal likes to be in charge. It will learn everything the hard way. You may also find that this is an expensive pet with frequent vet visits, medications, or behavior issues or a voracious appetite.

PET NUMBER 9: This is a wonderful and protective companion. They have old soul energy, and you'll feel like you connect on a different, deeper level.

Let's look at a few famous pets:

```
1        9 5      6 Soul Number (vowels)
L A S S  I E      5 Personality Number (consonants)
3    1 1          11/2 Destiny Number (total name letters)
```

Lassie is a loyal family member, with a need for adventure and has an intuitive sense second to none. Sensitive and nurturing, her rewards come through humanitarian efforts.

```
1        9 5          6 Soul Number (vowels)
G A R F  I E L D      11/2 Personality (consonants)
7   9 6      3 4      8 Destiny (total name numbers)
```

Garfield is a domesticated family member, smart and intuitive, wields a lot of power, and is an expensive pet, whether through vet bills, food costs, or damaging behavior!

Stay aware of the nicknames you use for your pet. They will grow into these vibrations as well!

Understanding Vibrations and Developing Intuition

As you practice Numerology, you will become more in tune and perceptive. You'll be more sensitive to and aware of the vibrations around you. At first you may want to showcase and boast about your developing gifts. Resist, as your new powers are best kept off the record until organically revealed.

Don't take your gifts for granted. Learn how to develop them responsibly. Everyone's intuition is unique. Some might call it by another name, such as a hunch, a stroke of genius, Spidey sense, inspiration, a flash of wisdom, a gut feeling, or following their heart. Intuition is a practical and spiritual intelligence that everyone can access if they try.

As you develop your intuition, you may want to practice meditation, which can help temper the emotional impulses within that may cloud your judgment and get in the way of your powers. Mindful meditation can help you simply observe your thoughts and feelings and help control emotional or ego-based impulses that can cloud judgment and be mistaken for intuition.

Different numbers will resonate with you differently. Some will always "click," and some you will struggle to understand and relate to. Remember there are no good or bad numbers, and your own Core Profile is not superior to anyone else's. Each has unique strengths and weaknesses. As you navigate situations and interactions with your newfound intuition, you don't need to announce what you experience and discover. Let it quietly guide you, and keep an open mind.

The numbers are your teachers, and soul growth is the ultimate goal. Pay attention, learn the lessons, and keep evolving.

7

TAROT, ASTROLOGY, AND CRYSTAL CONNECTIONS

In addition to Numerology, there are other meta-physical sciences that can guide you on your life path and deepen your intuition. Combining Numerology, Astrology, and the Tarot is a truly magical experience. These practices work harmoniously and complement one another, providing further insights. I've found that they rarely contradict each other.

While I am not a professional Astrologist or Tarot Reader, I have studied both and keep a close eye on the stars, the planets, and especially the moon. I use the Tarot to deliver clarity and on occasion provide confirmation for a reading. I'm also a certified Crystal Healer and love incorporating crystals into my readings.

Numerology can bring greater understanding to your personal Astrology or Tarot card readings. Through Numerology, the numbers on your Tarot cards will immediately have greater meaning to you, and you will begin to apply the meanings of the numbers to the Houses in Astrology, the degrees of the planets, and so much more.

Use these practices in tandem and they will only amplify each other and deepen your powers.

They help fill in the blanks and can illuminate divine communications, giving us new tools for understanding ourselves, interacting with others, connecting to the collective consciousness, and harnessing Universal wisdom.

It is also important to give credit to the other arts: I have often seen readers combine Numerology into their readings but rarely acknowledging it as the source of their enhanced findings. If you are ever asked for your birthday by an intuitive, they are harnessing some Numerological influence! Now you know.

What's My Zodiac Sign?

As we refer to Zodiac signs throughout this chapter, refer back to this handy chart.

Aries	Mar 21 – Apr 20	♈
Taurus	Apr 21 – May 20	♉
Gemini	May 21 – Jun 21	♊
Cancer	Jun 22 – Jul 22	♋
Leo	Jul 23 – Aug 23	♌
Virgo	Aug 24 – Sept 23	♍
Libra	Sept 24 – Oct 23	♎
Scorpio	Oct 24 – Nov 22	♏
Sagittarius	Nov 23 – Dec 21	♐
Capricorn	Dec 22 – Jan 20	♑
Aquarius	Jan 21 – Feb 18	♒
Pisces	Feb 19 – Mar 20	♓

Astrology & Numerology

Astrology and Numerology have a lot in common. Both are based on your birth date, both reveal and unlock your soul contract, and both reveal important themes, character traits, and potential lessons.

With 9 possible Life Path Numbers and 12 signs of the Zodiac, there are 108 possible combinations of unique personality types when combining Numerology and Astrology.

I won't get into the traits of all the signs of the Zodiac here. That's a whole other book—and there are many of them! (See Resources, page 147, for my recommendations.) Sometimes the Life Path Number and Zodiac sign blend well. For instance, if you are a Taurus with a Life Path 4, you won't have many surprises in your personality. You will be organized, rule abiding, and dutiful. Same is true if you are a Leo with a Life Path 1: You will be bold and confident.

Where things get a little more interesting (and complicated) is when there is no obvious compatability between the Zodiac sign and number. In this case, self-awareness is very important: The sign and number can either ground or intensify each other.

If you choose to study both Astrology and Numerology, combining these two powerful forces will become second nature when you read people.

WORKING WITH THE PLANETS

There are certain planetary events that we know will happen in Astrology at certain times. For instance, Mercury goes into retrograde three to four times per year. This is the planet that rules communications, technology, and travel. When it's in retrograde, it's a time to revisit, reflect, and revise things that require adjustment in our lives.

Anything you can put a "re-" in front of is a good activity for Mercury Retrograde. This way, instead of dreading when Mercury goes into retrograde, you can reframe your retrograde experience. Be aware of when it will occur, and use the time to *rest, reset, reflect, refresh, reevaluate, review, realign,* and *reboot.*

Going even further, you can apply your Personal Month (see page 83) to this challenging cycle to access guidance about where you should focus your energy and how you can move through retrograde gracefully. For example, if you are in Personal Month 8 during a Mercury Retrograde, you may want to *refinance* something or *return* a purchase (avoid shopping; you will likely *regret* what you buy later). If Mercury Retrograde falls in a Personal Month 6, it is a good time to *reconnect* with an old friend, *reconcile* with a family member, or *revisit* a *relationship* from the past.

Another example is your Saturn Return. This is the planet of karma and hard lessons, and it takes approximately 29.5 years to make its way around the sun.

When Saturn returns to the same Zodiac sign it was in when you were born, you will experience your Saturn Return, which lasts two and a half to three years. This is a period of change, difficult growth, and major beginning and endings. Synching your Saturn Return with your Personal Years will help you navigate this tricky period more smoothly. It is often a time of major changes.

The applications of this type of synchronized knowledge are endless. Apply it to your Birth Chart, Astrological Houses, and more.

WORKING WITH THE MOON

One of the easiest ways to meld Astrology with Numerology is to apply it to the Moon Cycles.

The New Moon is best used to manifest your goals and bring your wishes and dreams into reality. The Full Moon is the time to release and forgive. When you apply your Personal Year and Month to the Moon Cycle, you can consciously work with the special opportunities the moon brings us. For example, if you are in your Personal Month 1 of new beginnings on the day of the New Moon, your manifesting powers will be at their peak, and it is a perfect time to create a vision board and set goals. During the New Moon in your Personal Month or Year 4, you can focus on manifesting good health or becoming more organized. In 6 energy, focus on your family or home and in an 8 cycle on your career or finances. The natural synchronicity of the universe is so powerful.

Similarly, when you are in your Personal Month 9, the Full Moon is an optimal time for releasing, forgiving, and letting go. Why would you waste that natural energy? It's so important to utilize the cosmic forces at work all around us.

Tarot & Numerology

Coming to the Tarot with a basic knowledge of Numerology will help you more easily learn the cards and apply them to life. In fact, many Tarot teachers suggest this method as the foundation to unlocking the basics of the cards quickly.

Reading Tarot cards requires initiative, intuition, and dedication. The numbers on the cards and the symbolism of the imagery on the cards work together like wine and cheese, one enhancing the other.

When you draw Tarot cards, you can look for numerical patterns such as repeating numbers (111), progression of numbers (1, 2, 3), and regression of numbers (9, 8, 7). The numbers expand each card's meaning and the interpretation of a combination of cards.

MAJOR ARCANA

The Major Arcana in Tarot has 22 cards. Right away, we know that 22, a Master Number, is at the foundation of the deck. In Tarot, every card has a number on it, and these numbers correspond directly to the root number energies of Numerology.

Pay special attention to Tarot cards that equate to Karmic Debt, the 13/4, 14/5, 16/7, and 19/1. These all speak of transformation and overcoming:

- The 13th card, Death, Transition, and Rebirth, promises better things to come, such as overcoming the karma of laziness or procrastination.

- The 14th card, Temperance, holds energy for overindulgence, representing the addictive qualities the 14/5 debt reveals. Self-discipline and moderation are the lessons here.

- The 16th card, The Tower, represents a rise and fall with the promise to rebuild and come back better and stronger.

- The 19th card, The Sun, holds joy and promise and when reduced— (1+9) = 10—shows awareness of the lessons learned and the promise to begin with a clean slate.

When combined with Numerology, the numbers in the Major Arcana become infused with divine intelligence.

MINOR ARCANA

The Minor Arcana has 56 cards [(5+6)=11], another Master Number, speaking to illumination and intuition.

The numbers in the Minor Arcana merge character and features. Each element (or suit) has a card of 1 through 10. The four elements are:

- Pentacles (coins): finance, hard work, abundance, matters of the material

- Cups: feelings, emotions, psychic abilities

- Swords: communication, intellect, the overactive mind

- Wands: growth, new ideas, development

When reading these cards, combine the unique powers of the element with the Numerological meaning of the number shown.

For example, in Numerology the 8 is about finance and authority. So the 8 of Pentacles clearly predicts success in career and profiting from skill. The imagery of the card also shows someone diligently working.

We also know that the 5's energy rules chaos. So the 5 of Wands depicts confusion and struggle to get something accomplished.

The 1's, or Aces, all represent beginnings within the four elements.

There are many books dedicated to exploring what many call Astro-Numerology as well as Tarot and Numerology. Every system is slightly different and unique, often contradicting one another. Explore these different perspectives, use your intuition, and figure out which blend works for you.

Crystal Connections & Numerology

It would be as rare as the crystal alexandrite to meet someone interested in metaphysics who didn't also love crystals and stones!

In 2017, I added Certified Crystal Healer (CCH) to my metaphysical toolbox. This allows me to prescribe crystals that can assist clients with various emotional, mental, and physical challenges. Crystals can be powerful tools.

To sense crystal energy, hold a crystal in the palm of your left hand. Energy enters through the left side of the body and exits on the right. Upon doing this, some people feel heat or cold, and some feel a pulse or tingly sensation. Some stones have a very weighted or grounding impression, others watery and emotional. What you sense can be very subtle or extremely powerful.

If you are unable to sense crystal energy vibrationally, connect to the color. When you look at the stone, what does it make you feel? What emotions surface? Connect visually with the tones, imperfections, sparkle, rainbows, and inclusions of the crystal to sense their vibrations.

The stones that have the highest vibrations and tend to be easiest for most people to sense are moldavite, selenite and shungite.

Here are some of my common Numerology-based crystal prescriptions:

Crystal or Stone	Most Beneficial for Numbers	Emotional Healing
Amethyst	All Numbers	Offers protection, breaks negative attachments, works as an energetic vacuum cleaner, cleans and heals spaces and rooms, opens third eye
Rose Quartz	2, 6	Feels like a bubble bath for your soul, connects with your heart, attracts love relationships, calls in unconditional love, promotes joy and emotional healing
Sardonyx	2, 7	Improves mental discipline, relieves anxiety, promotes optimism and confidence, boosts happiness
Carnelian	3, 8	Sparks action, courage, confidence, creativity, and motivation, clarifies goals, is grounding
Ametrine	3, 5, 4, 8	Dissolves negativity, offers protection, helps break habits and addictions, promotes overcoming fear and procrastination, can also aid in weight loss
Apatite	1, 6, 2	Sparks joy; dissolves fear, anxiety, anger, and doubt; assists in letting go of people and things; aids in weight loss

Crystal or Stone	Most Beneficial for Numbers	Emotional Healing
Bronzite	All numbers	Promotes peace, harmony, forgiveness, and compassion; offers psychic protection and is grounding; transmutes negative energy and returns it to sender so that they can learn from it. Pair with tourmaline or obsidian.
Citrine	4, 8	Attracts wealth, health, happiness, and success; promotes self-confidence and empowerment; boosts manifestation, especially when combined with affirmations
Danburite	2, 6	Acts as energetic ladder, soothes emotions, releases worry and stress, promotes communication with Guides and Angels, helps ease misunderstandings, encourages patience and peace of mind
Diopside	4, 6, 7, 9	Boosts creativity, analytical skills, logic, and learning; provides emotional support; is empowering; soothes muscle aches

Crystal or Stone	Most Beneficial for Numbers	Emotional Healing
Imperial Topaz	1, 3, 7, 9	Unites desire and motivation, promotes learning and retaining information, builds confidence and self-love
Peridot	1, 8	Attracts abundance, health, and wealth; provides hope, vision, success; is helpful when starting new projects
Lepidolite	1, 5, 6, 9	The "friendship stone"; eases stress, mood swings, self-criticism, addictions, and worry
Scapolite	4, 9	Busts through procrastination; promotes achievement, motivation, self-discipline, willpower, and overcoming self-sabotage; releases karma, emotional baggage, and fear; creates change and forward movement
Selenite	All numbers	Breaks through blockages, enhances health and wellness, integrates right and left brain. This stone can be used to energetically clear other crystals and stones.

Crystals are a natural fit with your new consciousness.

Exploring their enchanting sparkle and natural magic can become a very rewarding—not to mention beautifying—venture.

Negative Ions

It sounds counterintuitive that something "negative" is good for you, but that is exactly the case with negative ions. These beneficial ions are found in clean air—think nature, mountains, the ocean, and waterfalls. Negative ions increase serotonin, alleviate depression, relieve stress, boost energy, promote deep sleep, and have numerous other health benefits.

The crystals selenite and Himalayan salt give off negative ions. I recommend keeping a Himalayan salt lamp in your home (these are easy to find online), preferably placed near electronics or computers to combat the electromagnetic fields. *(Be sure to keep these away from pets, as they can cause issues if ingested.)*

Selenite is also cleansing. I use it to cleanse everything from Tarot card decks and crystals to jewelry and money. You can give these stones a boost by charging them in sunlight every two to three months. Never get them wet.

Your Metaphysical Toolbox

The more you learn about the world of metaphysics, the more you can develop your own unique interpretations to layer into your readings and insights.

The helpful chart below shows which Zodiac sign, Tarot representations, crystals, and colors correlate to the numbers 1 through 9 and Master Numbers in Numerology.

For example, 6 energy is all about love, Venus is the planet of love, and its Tarot representative is the Lovers VI card as well as the Devil XV card (because of the angel/devil quality of the 6 as discussed in chapter 2) and the 6's in the Minor Arcana, which play out as follows:

6 OF PENTACLES: sharing the wealth; 6's are known for their compassion and generosity.

6 OF SWORDS: leaving sorrow behind (the 6 has no shortage of emotional baggage).

6 OF CUPS: representation of friends, family, childhood, and hometown.

6 OF WANDS: coming home to success, or the arrival of friends and family.

In the Zodiac, we find 6 energy in various signs that share character traits. For instance, Libras and 6's are both idealistic and value harmony while Virgos and 6's are both perfectionists.

The Number 1

Ruled by:	The sun
Astrological Equal:	Leo, Aries
Crystal:	Ruby, garnet
Color:	Red, flame, burgundy, cardinal, gold
Tarot Representation:	The Magician I & Aces of the Minor Arcana Wheel of Fortune X, The Sun XIX

The Numbers 2 & 11

Ruled by:	The Moon
Astrological Equal:	Libra, Cancer
Crystal:	Moonstone, quartz
Color:	Orange, peach, gold
Tarot Representation:	High Priestess II, the 2's of the Minor Arcana
	Justice XI, Judgment XX

The Number 3

Ruled by:	Jupiter
Astrological Equal:	Sagittarius, Pisces, Leo
Crystal:	Turquoise, amazonite, topaz
Color:	Yellow, gold, lemon
Tarot Representation:	The Empress III, the 3's of the Minor Arcana
	The Hanged Man XII, The World XXI

The Numbers 4 & 22

Ruled by:	Saturn
Astrological Equal:	Taurus, Virgo, Capricorn
Crystal:	Jade, emerald
Color:	Greens
Tarot Representation:	The Emperor IV, the 4's of the Minor Arcana
	Death XIII

The Number 5

Ruled by:	Mercury, Uranus
Astrological Equal:	Gemini, Aquarius, Sagittarius
Crystal:	Aquamarine, turquoise, fluorite
Color:	Turquoise, shades of green-blue
Tarot Representation:	The Hierophant V, the 5's of the Minor Arcana
	Temperance XIV

The Numbers 6 & 33

Ruled by:	Venus
Astrological Equal:	Taurus, Libra, Cancer, Virgo
Crystal:	Sapphire, lapis lazuli, rose quartz
Color:	Royal blue, indigo
Tarot Representation:	The Lovers VI, the 6's of the Minor Arcana The Devil XV

The Number 7

Ruled by:	Neptune
Astrological Equal:	Pisces, Scorpio
Crystal:	Amethyst, alexandrite
Color:	Purple, violet
Tarot Representation:	The Chariot VII, the 7's of the Minor Arcana The Tower XVI

The Number 8

Ruled by:	Saturn
Astrological Equal:	Capricorn, Leo, Libra
Crystal:	Citrine, aventurine, pyrite
Color:	Rose, pink
Tarot Representation:	Strength VIII, the 8's of the Minor Arcana The Star XVII

The Number 9

Ruled by:	Mars
Astrological Equal:	Scorpio, Capricorn, Aquarius
Crystal:	Opal, smoky quartz
Color:	White, black, pearl
Tarot Representation:	Hermit IX, the 9's of the Minor Arcana The Moon XVIII

Now that you've filled up your metaphysical toolbox, let's look at how numbers appear in your everyday life and how you can apply your new Numerology knowledge.

8

Now that you have dipped your toe into the shallow end of the deep, deep waters of Numerology, I encourage you to keep exploring, learning, and reading. Continued curiosity is critical to your success. In addition to reading this book, getting a professional reading can be a moving and worthwhile experience. You will be able to ask questions and get clarification on certain aspects of your profile. As you read, research, and observe, keep a journal or spreadsheet of your findings, Birth and Name Charts, and experiences. Over time you'll develop your own unique style.

Numbers Everywhere

Addresses, phone numbers, license plates, receipts, account numbers—these all hold numerical energy. You can explore and examine any number that catches your curiosity! (As you might already be able to tell, Numerology can quickly become an obsession.)

Movies, television, and books will be changed forever as you start paying closer attention to all the clues buried in characters, dialogue, and plot. Addresses of fictional houses, numbers scribbled on notes in scenes, and other numbers you might have overlooked before will add detail to a story. I often wish that reality shows revealed the birth dates of their participants!

The news consistently sends me down the Google rabbit hole. I find myself looking for alleged criminals' birth dates, the anniversaries of famous Hollywood couples, the date of an election, or the birthday of a new royal baby. In addition to being fun, these events are gold mines for numerical learning.

To practice and keep things interesting, look for numbers when you travel: your seat number on a train or airplane, your flight number, the number for your bus route, and your hotel room can all foreshadow the experience you'll have on your journey.

Numerology comes in handy when considering contractors, doctors, or job candidates, allowing you apply your new knowledge to hiring decisions, projects, your health, and more. Seek out certain numerical attributes for certain roles, such as a 1 (naturally healing hands) for a massage therapist, a 4 (loves systems and follows rules) for your accountant, or a 6 (rules, education, and learning) in a teacher.

I encourage you to observe numbers everywhere, but know that Numerology can become an obsession. Always use Numerology to complement your life and offer divine insight and guidance.

I Keep Seeing This Number!

Now that the Universe knows you are becoming fluent in the language of numbers, it will speak to you in a unique way. It is up to you to be aware and pick up on the messages being sent your way. Pay attention to the signs! 11:11 invites you to walk through a spiritual gateway; numerical messages are asking you to take action.

Here is a basic rundown of some of the most common numerical patterns people notice and what they mean:

111	Beginnings, time to take action
222	Harmony, relationships, cooperation, patience
333	Communication, creativity, emotions
444	Angel number, divine support from source energy
555	Change, movement, shift, travel
777	Spirit, investigation, expertise, self-care
10:10	The "new" 11:11; the cipher or 0 amplifies the 1, representing continued spiritual awakening and development of intuition
11:11	A doorway to spiritual enlightenment, enhanced intuition
12:34	Progress, advancement

Whenever you spot your own birthday, it means you are on the right path and unseen forces are working in your favor. Seeing a friend or loved one's birthday might signify that they need your help or support. If you notice the birthday of a deceased loved one, it means they are giving you guidance or letting you know they are with you.

Paying attention to these signs and messages can help you avoid a spiritual 2x4 smacking you across the head. If you ignore what the Universe is telling you, its messages will become less subtle. Eventually they will turn into excruciating lessons and you will have to course correct. It's much better to take action on subtle messages or warnings than wait for a painful event that forces you to change.

Readings for Others

When you start doing readings for others, whether your family, friends, or clients, you will move through the five numbers of their Core Profile, and there are some important things to keep in mind.

Always start with the Life Path Number, and explain to your participant why it is the most important number in their profile. Then, move on to the Soul Number, to reveal what their heart wants: This is the private, more intimate side of them that only those very close to them get to see. Touch on compatibility by explaining Soul Stress Numbers (page 114).

From there, look at the Personality, Destiny, and Birthday Numbers. These all have a profound effect on career and how one makes a living. Discuss the special gifts, talents, and abilities this numerical energy grants them.

Follow with the Attitude Number, explaining this is where first impressions and judgments are born. Finish with the Maturity Number, which becomes more relevant depending on the person's age.

While you are doing the reading, pay special attention to the placement and influence of each number. If there are repeating numbers in the chart, discuss those intensities. Repetition can significantly change the meaning of the information you relay.

Explain Karmic Lessons and Debt as they are revealed, and always offer gentle guidance about how to learn lessons and pay the cosmic bank. Empower them with the tools to resolve karma during their lifetime.

Close with the cycles and timing of their Personal Years, Months, and Days in order to give them awareness of the opportunities, possibilities, and challenges that may come their way.

BE SENSITIVE AND RESPECTFUL

Doing readings for others comes with immense responsibility. Think about who usually asks for a reading—generally, people seek help in times of despair or when at an important crossroads. They are looking to the spiritual world for guidance. Consider it an honor and a privilege to provide guidance during such times.

Clients, friends, and family might make important decisions based on the information and insights you provide. Because of this, you must be careful with your words and never project your personal feelings, judgments, or opinions into the reading. Remember that you are just a conduit for the intelligence the numbers provide.

Keep it positive. Avoid creating self-fulfilling prophecies for your clients or friends. For example, if you find markers for divorce in a chart, don't doom the person to give up on a relationship as soon as it gets hard (there's always room for interpretation: this is also the marker for someone who is widowed or has lost a parent at a young age). Instead, explain they may experience some harsh lessons around love. You never know exactly how the numbers will play out in another person's life. As the always inspiring Maya Angelou said, "Words are things, I'm convinced. You must be careful." You cannot undo the power of a word once spoken. Bring kindness, empathy, and compassion; these traits will be some of your greatest assets as a reader.

If you choose to showcase your new knowledge as a party trick, be respectful of the science. Always make sure you are accurate and have a clear mind (math and alcohol don't usually mix well). Many intuitives believe that if the gift is abused or used in the wrong way, their abilities will be decreased or even blocked.

Some clients will take everything to heart; others will struggle against it. Free will is always involved, and people will heal only when they are ready.

I cannot emphasize this enough: Ground your energy. You do not want to take on someone else's problems or toxic energy, so implement boundaries. There are many effective techniques and crystals that offer protection. Continue with your own research and find a method that works for you.

To quote Numerologist Hans Decoz, "Numerology is a difficult, but intensely rewarding profession." Motivate, inspire, elevate, provide insight, and always tell the truth, and your readings will be fabulous!

DEVELOPING YOUR INTUITION

Your intuition will continue to evolve and expand along with your awareness and confidence. Understanding and developing intuition is deeply personal and happens differently for everyone.

Early in my Numerology career, I was taught the concept of "blah"—basically, receiving a very strong message that you blurt or "blah" out (which stands for "bring love and healing"). This phenomenon has created some of my most meaningful and heartfelt connections with clients. Several stories come to mind, but I'll share just one:

That nagging message came to me as the words "blue plaid shirt, blue plaid shirt." I tried to dismiss it, but it was relentless, as messages from the Universe tend to be. Eventually, I asked the client the significance of this image. They had no immediate answer, so I continued on with the reading. By the end of our time together, her face lit up and she ran out to her truck to get something to show me, a program from her father-in-law's memorial. It had a photo of him in a blue plaid shirt.

I still get chills when I think about how emotional this was for her.

Finding the balance between kindness, honesty, and censorship will be crucial. Check your ego, keep everything confidential, and deliver your intuitive readings with compassion and love.

CRACKING THE CODE

Whether you choose to reveal your new ability is up to you. People can get strangely secretive about their birth date (or even provide inaccurate information) when they feel you could reveal something that they'd rather keep private. With experience, you will likely know when this is the case. Never push someone to share their numbers with you. Always be open to learning, respect boundaries, and keep an open mind.

Eventually they'll understand what you know after reading this book: that life can be easier, decisions and timing less confusing, and relationships more harmonious, and greater opportunities can be seized through Numerology.

Embrace the magic of the Universe. I've often said that if everyone had just a little Numerology in their lives, the world would be a more magical, understanding, and compassionate place.

Congratulations on your newfound wisdom.

RESOURCES & REFERENCES

Bell, Pamela, and Simon Jordan. *Astronumerology*. New York, NY: Avon Books, 1998.

Boland, Yasmin. *Astrology: A Guide to Understanding Your Birth Chart*. Carlsbad, CA: Hay House, 2016.

Decoz, Hans, and Tom Monte. *Numerology: The Key to Your Inner Self*. New York, NY: Penguin Group, 1994.

Dodge, Ellen. *Numerology Has Your Number*. New York, NY: Simon & Schuster, 1988.

Goodwin, Matthew Oliver. *Numerology: The Complete Guide*. Franklin Lakes, NJ: The Career Press, 1981.

Hicks, Esther and Jerry. *Ask and It Is Given*. Carlsbad, CA: Hay House, 2004.

Jordan, Juno. *Numerology: The Romance in Your Name*. Camarillo, CA: DeVorss & Company, 1984.

Lagerquist, PhD, Kay, and Lisa Lenard. *Numerology, 2nd Edition*. New York, NY: Penguin Group, 2004.

Lawrence, Shirley Blackwell. *Behind Numerology*. North Hollywood, CA: Newcastle Publishing, 1989.

Lawrence, Shirley. *Exploring Numerology: Life by the Numbers*. Franklin Lakes, NJ: The Career Press, 2003.

Shine, Norman. *Numerology: Your Character and Future Revealed in Numbers*. New York, NY: Simon & Schuster, 1994.

Simmons, Robert, and Naisha Ahsian. *The Book of Stones*. East Montpellier, VT: Heaven & Earth Publishing, 2005.

www.astrology.com

www.astrostyle.com

www.biddytarot.com

www.joyofnumerology.com

www.moonology.com

www.numerologist.com

www.worldnumerology.com

INDEX